FEDERAL REAL PROPERTY MANAGEMENT

PARTNERSHIP OPTIONS AND ENHANCED USE LEASING

GOVERNMENT PROCEDURES AND OPERATIONS

GOVERNMENT PROCEDURES AND OPERATIONS

FEDERAL REAL PROPERTY MANAGEMENT

PARTNERSHIP OPTIONS AND ENHANCED USE LEASING

AARON F. DARBY
EDITOR

nova publishers

New York

Copyright © 2014 by Nova Science Publishers, Inc.

For permission to use material from this book please contact us:
Telephone 631-231-7269; Fax 631-231-8175
Web Site: http://www.novapublishers.com

NOTICE TO THE READER

The Publisher has taken reasonable care in the preparation of this book, but makes no expressed or implied warranty of any kind and assumes no responsibility for any errors or omissions. No liability is assumed for incidental or consequential damages in connection with or arising out of information contained in this book. The Publisher shall not be liable for any special, consequential, or exemplary damages resulting, in whole or in part, from the readers' use of, or reliance upon, this material. Any parts of this book based on government reports are so indicated and copyright is claimed for those parts to the extent applicable to compilations of such works.

Independent verification should be sought for any data, advice or recommendations contained in this book. In addition, no responsibility is assumed by the publisher for any injury and/or damage to persons or property arising from any methods, products, instructions, ideas or otherwise contained in this publication.

This publication is designed to provide accurate and authoritative information with regard to the subject matter covered herein. It is sold with the clear understanding that the Publisher is not engaged in rendering legal or any other professional services. If legal or any other expert assistance is required, the services of a competent person should be sought. FROM A DECLARATION OF PARTICIPANTS JOINTLY ADOPTED BY A COMMITTEE OF THE AMERICAN BAR ASSOCIATION AND A COMMITTEE OF PUBLISHERS.

Additional color graphics may be available in the e-book version of this book.

Library of Congress Cataloging-in-Publication Data

ISBN: 978-1-63321-219-0

Published by Nova Science Publishers, Inc. † New York

CONTENTS

PREFACE

This book provides an overview of key policy and legal issues pertaining to PPPs for purposes of federal real property management. The book also discusses the potential for collocation and the factors that can affect that potential; the possible benefits of collocation; the the challenges associated with collocation, and what solutions, if any, can mitigate these challenges; the extent to which agencies attribute the full benefits and costs of their enhanced use leases (EUL) in their assessments of their EUL programs; and the experiences of agencies in using their EUL authority.

Chapter 1 – While public-private partnerships (PPPs) have long been used to manage real property, congressional interest in PPPs has recently increased due to the large number of underutilized and excess buildings owned by federal agencies, as well as sequestration and other spending constraints. There is no single, accepted definition of *public-private partnership*, and PPPs can be structured in many ways. However, for purposes of this report, a PPP is an agreement whereby a nonfederal entity acquires the right to use a real property owned or controlled by a federal agency—typically through a long-term lease—in exchange for redeveloping or renovating that property (or other property). In many cases, the agency and the nonfederal entity share the net cash flow or savings that result from the agreement. The term *real property* is defined by the Federal Management Regulation as any interest in land under the control of a federal agency except the public domain; lands reserved or dedicated for national forest or park purposes; minerals in lands withdrawn or reserved from the public domain; other lands withdrawn or reserved from the public domain; and crops separated from the land.

The process of forming a PPP typically begins when a federal agency identifies real property that could provide greater benefits to the government if it were redeveloped or renovated. The agency then works with nonfederal partners to see if a redevelopment strategy could be devised that provides the agency with the benefits it seeks, and the nonfederal partner with financial returns sufficient to cover the risk of investing in the property. The redevelopment strategy and method of financing are closely linked. The former refers specifically to the work that the nonfederal partner agrees to undertake, while the latter is a combination of the revenue generated from the improved space and, in some cases, savings realized by reduced operating costs. Financial benefits to the government may also include a division of property cash flows. Two common redevelopment and financing structures entail (1) leasing property to a developer, which then constructs a new facility on the land and subleases the facility; and (2) giving a developer excess real property in exchange for the developer building a facility for the agency on other land that the agency owns.

Federal law is generally silent as to PPPs, *per se*, particularly PPPs for purposes of improving or disposing of federal real property. A number of states have laws that define *public-private partnership*, and expressly authorize one or more state agencies (often, the Department of Transportation) to enter PPPs in general or for specific purposes (e.g., toll roads). With certain narrow exceptions (e.g., P.L. 106-407), federal law has no comparable provisions. Instead, those agencies which have, to date, entered agreements that could be characterized as PPPs have typically done so under their authority (1) to lease, otherwise convey, or permit the use of federal real property; and (2) to enter procurement contracts, particularly energy savings performance contracts (ESPCs). While the authorities as to procurement contracts often apply to all executive branch agencies, those as to leases generally apply only to specific agencies and properties, and sometimes only to agreements entered into for specific purposes. Thus, there is considerable variability in the types of PPPs that agencies may enter, and some uncertainties as to the legal requirements to which such partnerships are subject.

When contemplating expanded use of PPPs, Congress may wish to consider the limited information available about existing authorities that may permit landholding agencies to enter PPPs, and whether and how these authorities are currently being utilized. Congress may also wish to consider agencies' capabilities to enter into and oversee performance of these arguably complicated arrangements; agencies' authority to retain and use any net proceeds from PPPs; and the interplay between PPPs and current processes for disposing of excess property.

Chapter 2 – GAO designated the federal government's management of its nearly 400,000 real property assets as high-risk in part because of overreliance on leasing and the retention of excess facilities. Real property management is coordinated nationally by the FRPC—an association of landholding agencies chaired by the Deputy Director for Management of the Office of Management and Budget (OMB). To explore the potential to reduce leasing by better utilizing owned properties, GAO was asked to examine: (1) the potential for collocation and the factors that can affect that potential, (2) the possible benefits of collocation, and (3) the challenges associated with collocation, and what solutions, if any, can mitigate these challenges. GAO reviewed property data and documents from eight of the largest property-holding agencies; laws, regulations and guidance; and prior GAO reports. GAO also analyzed eight case study markets of varying size and federal agency presence, and interviewed agency officials.

Chapter 3 – The federal government owns underutilized properties that are costly to operate, yet challenges exist to closing and disposing of them. To obtain value from these properties, some agencies have used EULs, which are generally long-term agreements to lease property from the federal government in exchange for cash or non-cash consideration. However, agencies also incur costs for EUL programs. The authors have previously reported that agencies should include all costs associated with programs' activities when assessing their values. This report addresses (1) the extent to which agencies attribute the full benefits and costs of their EULs in their assessments of their EUL programs and (2) the experiences of agencies in using their EUL authority.

GAO reviewed property data and documents from the largest civilian federal real property agencies including four agencies that use EULs—VA, NASA, the Department of State, and the Department of Agriculture—and applicable laws, and regulations and guidance. GAO visited nine sites where agencies were using EULs.

Chapter 4 – Many federal agencies hold real property that they do not need, including property that is underutilized or excess. Such properties present significant potential risks to federal agencies because they are costly to maintain and could be put to more cost-beneficial uses or sold to generate revenue for the government. The authors first designated federal real property management as a high-risk area in January 2003 due to longstanding problems with underutilized and excess property, among other things. After their high-risk designation, President George W. Bush added real property management to the President's Management Agenda and directed that the Federal Real Property Profile (FRPP) be established as a comprehensive database of real property under the control and custody of executive branch agencies, with agencies required to report on their real property assets each year. The President also established a goal of disposing of $15 billion in unneeded real property assets by 2015 to encourage agencies to right-size their portfolios by eliminating unneeded property.

In: Federal Real Property Management
Editor: Aaron F. Darby
ISBN: 978-1-63321-219-0
© 2014 Nova Science Publishers, Inc.

Chapter 1

PUBLIC-PRIVATE PARTNERSHIPS FOR PURPOSES OF FEDERAL REAL PROPERTY MANAGEMENT[*]

Garrett Hatch and Kate M. Manuel

SUMMARY

While public-private partnerships (PPPs) have long been used to manage real property, congressional interest in PPPs has recently increased due to the large number of underutilized and excess buildings owned by federal agencies, as well as sequestration and other spending constraints. There is no single, accepted definition of *public-private partnership*, and PPPs can be structured in many ways. However, for purposes of this report, a PPP is an agreement whereby a nonfederal entity acquires the right to use a real property owned or controlled by a federal agency—typically through a long-term lease—in exchange for redeveloping or renovating that property (or other property). In many cases, the agency and the nonfederal entity share the net cash flow or savings that result from the agreement. The term *real property* is defined by the Federal Management Regulation as any interest in land under the control of a federal agency except the public domain; lands reserved or dedicated for national forest or park purposes; minerals in lands

---

[*] This is an edited, reformatted and augmented version of Congressional Research Service publication, No. R43337, dated December 12, 2013.

withdrawn or reserved from the public domain; other lands withdrawn or reserved from the public domain; and crops separated from the land.

The process of forming a PPP typically begins when a federal agency identifies real property that could provide greater benefits to the government if it were redeveloped or renovated. The agency then works with nonfederal partners to see if a redevelopment strategy could be devised that provides the agency with the benefits it seeks, and the nonfederal partner with financial returns sufficient to cover the risk of investing in the property. The redevelopment strategy and method of financing are closely linked. The former refers specifically to the work that the nonfederal partner agrees to undertake, while the latter is a combination of the revenue generated from the improved space and, in some cases, savings realized by reduced operating costs. Financial benefits to the government may also include a division of property cash flows. Two common redevelopment and financing structures entail (1) leasing property to a developer, which then constructs a new facility on the land and subleases the facility; and (2) giving a developer excess real property in exchange for the developer building a facility for the agency on other land that the agency owns.

Federal law is generally silent as to PPPs, *per se*, particularly PPPs for purposes of improving or disposing of federal real property. A number of states have laws that define *public-private partnership*, and expressly authorize one or more state agencies (often, the Department of Transportation) to enter PPPs in general or for specific purposes (e.g., toll roads). With certain narrow exceptions (e.g., P.L. 106-407), federal law has no comparable provisions. Instead, those agencies which have, to date, entered agreements that could be characterized as PPPs have typically done so under their authority (1) to lease, otherwise convey, or permit the use of federal real property; and (2) to enter procurement contracts, particularly energy savings performance contracts (ESPCs). While the authorities as to procurement contracts often apply to all executive branch agencies, those as to leases generally apply only to specific agencies and properties, and sometimes only to agreements entered into for specific purposes. Thus, there is considerable variability in the types of PPPs that agencies may enter, and some uncertainties as to the legal requirements to which such partnerships are subject.

When contemplating expanded use of PPPs, Congress may wish to consider the limited information available about existing authorities that may permit landholding agencies to enter PPPs, and whether and how these authorities are currently being utilized. Congress may also wish to consider agencies' capabilities to enter into and oversee performance of these arguably complicated arrangements; agencies' authority to retain and use any net proceeds from PPPs; and the interplay between PPPs and current processes for disposing of excess property.

While public-private partnerships (PPPs) have long been used to manage real property,[1] congressional interest in PPPs has recently increased due to the large number of underutilized and excess buildings owned by federal agencies, as well as sequestration and other spending constraints. According to a report on federal real property holdings in FY2010, the government's portfolio included 71,000 underutilized buildings and 6,700 excess buildings, which cost a combined $1.66 billion to operate and maintain.[2] Disposing of these buildings through the "standard" processes, described below, imposes its own costs—and can take years—as agencies must comply with various statutory mandates pertaining to environmental remediation, historic preservation, and "public benefit" conveyances. Moreover, these costs in operating, maintaining, or disposing of property are currently being incurred at a time when agencies generally have fewer appropriated funds at their disposal due to sequestration and tightening budgets. Annual appropriations for real property activities at the General Services Administration (GSA), for example, have decreased by more than half a billion dollars from FY2010 ($8.54 billion)[3] to FY2012 ($8.02 billion).[4] Taken together, these factors have prompted increased interest in PPPs, which generally rely upon nonfederal entities to finance redevelopment and, in some cases, disposal of federal real property.

There is no single, accepted definition of *public-private partnership*, and PPPs can be structured in many ways. However, for purposes of this report, a PPP is an agreement whereby a nonfederal entity acquires the right to use real property owned or controlled by a federal agency—typically through a long-term lease—in exchange for redeveloping or renovating that property (or other property). In many cases, the agency and the nonfederal entity share the net cash flow or savings that result from the agreement. The term *real property* is defined by the Federal Management Regulation as any interest in land, together with any fixtures thereon, under the control of a federal agency *except:* (1) the public domain; (2) lands reserved or dedicated for national forest or park purposes; (3) minerals in lands withdrawn or reserved from the public domain that are suitable for disposition under the public land mining and mineral leasing laws; (4) certain other lands withdrawn or reserved from the public domain; and (5) any crops designated for disposition by severance and removal from the land.[5]

This report provides an overview of key policy and legal issues pertaining to PPPs for purposes of federal real property management. It begins by discussing the current processes whereby federal agencies maintain and dispose of real property, as these processes help explain the appeal of PPPs. The report then discusses how PPPs are commonly structured, agencies' authority to enter PPPs, and the legal requirements to which PPPs may be subject. It concludes with considerations for Congress, such as agencies' capabilities to enter into and oversee performance of these arguably complicated arrangements.

BACKGROUND

Current interest in PPPs arises, in part, as a result of the "standard" processes agencies use to dispose of real property that they no longer need due to changes in their functions and missions. As a general rule, when agencies no longer need particular properties, they must dispose of these properties through statutorily prescribed processes, described below, that can be cumbersome and costly. Agencies frequently must spend appropriated funds to operate and maintain properties they no longer need, and pay costs associated with their disposal. PPPs potentially enable federal agencies to rely upon nonfederal entities to finance the operation and maintenance of such properties, or to exchange these properties for other real property or services.

Changes in Agency Missions, Changes in Property Portfolios

Federal agencies acquire and maintain a range of real property assets to help them fulfill specific functions and missions. The Department of Energy (DOE), for example, owns more than a dozen laboratories which support its mission of promoting scientific and technological innovation through research, and the Department of Veterans Affairs (VA) owns over a hundred hospitals which support its mission of providing health care to veterans and their families. Agencies also own thousands of properties they use for office space, barracks, family housing units, and warehouses.[6] In total, the government owned more than 306,000 buildings at the end of FY2012.[7]

Over time, agency portfolios change, sometimes significantly. Agencies may restructure their real property portfolios, for example, as their needs change. The Department of Defense (DOD) closed numerous bases over the past two decades as part of its effort to restructure America's military forces to meet national security threats in the post-Cold War environment.[8] Agencies may also consolidate their real property holdings in order to achieve operational benefits. The Department of Homeland Security (DHS), for example, is currently in the process of consolidating personnel from several locations in the Washington, DC, area, into a new headquarters at the West Campus of St. Elizabeth's Hospital—a move which DHS believes will improve communication and coordination across its administrative components.[9] Agencies may also transfer personnel from one location to another in order to reduce costs. The Bureau of Public Debt (BPD), for example, plans to relocate 450 employees from Hyattsville, MD, to Parkersburg, WV, potentially allowing BPD to realize an estimated $36 million in savings over five years.[10]

When agency personnel are relocated, they leave behind empty space in the buildings their employees once occupied. In some cases, entire properties may no longer be needed by an agency, in which case those properties are designated as *excess*.[11] In other cases, an agency may choose to retain property that it only partially occupies, in which case the property is considered *underutilized*.[12] The frequent shifting of agency staff between buildings has left the government with a substantial amount of excess and underutilized space, which can be costly to maintain. As previously noted, according to a report on federal real property holdings in FY2010, the government's portfolio included 71,000 underutilized buildings and 6,700 excess buildings, which cost a combined $1.66 billion to operate and maintain.[13] Moreover, the number of excess and underutilized buildings is not steadily declining, but fluctuates over time, sometimes increasing by hundreds of properties a year. For example, the government ended FY2008 with 43,360 underutilized and 10,140 excess buildings in its portfolio, but ended FY2009 with 45,190 underutilized and 10,327 excess buildings—a net increase of 2,017 unneeded properties.[14] The ongoing cost of maintaining thousands of properties that are needed only in part, or not at all, is one of the primary reasons the Government Accountability Office (GAO) has included federal real property management on its "high-risk" list since 2003.[15]

"Standard" Disposal Process Can Be Cumbersome and Costly

One reason agencies hold so many unneeded properties is that the real property disposal process can be cumbersome and costly. The steps in the "standard" disposal process are prescribed by statute.[16] Agencies must first offer to transfer properties they do not need (i.e., excess properties) to other federal agencies, which generally must pay market value for excess properties they wish to acquire.[17] Excess properties that are not acquired by federal agencies (known as *surplus properties*) must then be offered to state and local governments, and qualified nonprofits, for use in accomplishing "public purposes" specified in statute, such as creating public parks or providing services to the homeless.[18] Agencies may convey surplus properties to state and local governments, and qualified nonprofits, for public benefit at less than fair market value—even at no cost.[19] Surplus properties not conveyed for public benefit are then available for sale, or are demolished if the property cannot be sold due to its condition or location.[20]

Agencies have consistently argued that these statutory requirements slow down the disposition process, compelling them to incur operating costs for months—sometimes years—while the properties are being screened.[21] Real property officials at the VA have said the McKinney-Vento Act (P.L. 100-77)—which generally mandates that surplus property be screened for use by organizations that assist the homeless—can add as much as two years to the disposal process.[22] Because public benefit conveyance requirements are prescribed by statute, agencies generally may not skip screening, even for surplus properties that could not be conveyed anyway.[23] Statutes pertaining to environmental remediation and historic preservation can also add time to the process. It may take agencies years of study to assess the potential environmental consequences of a proposed disposal, and to develop and implement an abatement plan, as required by law.[24] Similarly, the National Historic Preservation Act requires agencies to plan their disposal actions so as to minimize the harm they cause to historic properties, which may require additional procedures, such as consulting with historic preservation groups at the state, local, and federal levels.[25] Agencies that wish to demolish vacant buildings face demolition and cleanup costs that, at times, exceed the cost of maintaining the property—at least in the short run—which may encourage real property managers to retain a property rather than dispose of it.[26] Further, some agencies have found their disposal efforts complicated by the involvement of stakeholders with competing agendas. The Department of the Interior (DOI) has said that its efforts to dispose of some of its unneeded real property can be complicated by the competing concerns of local and state governments, and historic preservation offices, as well as by political factors.[27]

PPPs as Alternative Means to Develop or Dispose of Property

In an effort to reduce the government's inventory of excess and underutilized properties, committees have held hearings during the 113th Congress on federal real property management and Members have introduced several bills that would reform the disposal process.[28] While many of these proposals have wide scope, there has been specific interest in expanding the use of PPPs. Proponents of PPPs have identified a number of potential benefits of such agreements, including that PPPs may enable agencies to finance real property activities—such as repairs and renovations—they do not have the funds to undertake. The risks and limitations associated with PPPs, in contrast, may be less well understood due, in part, to the various legal authorities that agencies rely upon in entering PPPs, and uncertainties regarding the legal requirements to which PPPs are subject.

Potential Benefits of PPPs

PPPs would appear to offer federal agencies numerous benefits, including reduced operating costs; repaired and modernized space; decreased maintenance and repair backlogs; and increased revenue. This is because, regardless of how specific PPPs are structured (see "PPP Structures," below), the contributions of each partner are generally the same: the federal government provides real property—buildings, space within buildings, land, or structures[29]—and the nonfederal partner provides capital for improvements to the property. The real property the government provides is typically underutilized or excess, and may include undeveloped land. These properties are often in suboptimal condition and in need of costly repairs. Their poor condition is due in part to their age—underutilized and excess properties are often among the oldest properties in an agency's portfolio. Many unneeded DOD buildings were originally constructed in the 1940s and 1950s, for example, in response to the military needs of World War II and the Cold War. Similarly, many unneeded facilities held by VA were built to treat soldiers who served in the military many decades ago, including buildings that date back to the Civil War. St. Elizabeth's Hospital, the new headquarters for the Department of Homeland Security (DHS), was built in 1855.

Underutilized and excess properties are also in poor condition because they have not been a priority for reinvestment. Agencies do not have sufficient funds in any given year to meet all of their real property needs, and when comparing the benefits of investing in expensive repairs of aging buildings (e.g., replacing obsolete electrical systems, or repairing roofs that leak), or acquiring new space that can help the agency better fulfill its mission, agencies generally prioritize the latter. With the acquisition of new space, agency personnel move out of older properties, rendering them even less valuable to the agency and less likely to receive needed repairs. As a result, the government holds thousands of properties it does not need and cannot afford to maintain, but which are in poor condition and therefore more difficult to dispose of. It has been estimated, for example, that VA would need to spend about $3 billion to repair the buildings in its portfolio rated in "poor" or "critical" condition—56% of which were vacant or underutilized, and therefore might be candidates for disposal.[30] Not surprisingly, underutilized and vacant properties are often a net cost to the government. Operating expenses for unneeded buildings continue to accrue, even if there are no tenants—and hence no revenue. When there are tenants, aging, inefficient systems are costly to run. Energy costs in older buildings are higher, for example, because such buildings have heating and cooling systems that are several generations old.

Despite these factors, nonfederal partners may see an opportunity to generate a profit, and therefore be willing to invest in a PPP. While underutilized and excess properties are often in poor condition, they may be in desirable locations where rental rates are high. The nonfederal partner may renovate the property and be able to recoup its costs through subleasing the improved space. Similarly, the nonfederal partner may see opportunities in the market for a particular type of space which it could provide through construction or renovation. There might be a strong demand for hospital space in a local market, for example, and a nonfederal partner might conclude that it would be a relatively low-risk investment to construct a new medical facility on undeveloped federal land in that area. In other cases, a nonfederal partner might have expertise in a particular type of renovation, such as installing energy efficient wastewater systems, and enter into an agreement that pays for the costs of such renovations through the savings in operating costs. The nonfederal partner might also be able to renovate unneeded space in an older building and make it more mission-effective for the agency that holds it. For example, an agency may not have the funds to upgrade the electrical system in an underutilized building in order to take advantage of new technology. A nonfederal partner might upgrade the electrical system in the entire building as part of its renovation and retain the rights to sublease the unoccupied space, while sharing the revenue with the landholding agency. In short, nonfederal partners with access to capital and real property expertise are often able to find ways to monetize assets that the government cannot, particularly under current fiscal constraints.

Potential Risks and Limitations

Despite providing numerous potential benefits to federal agencies and their partners, PPPs are not without their risks and limitations. These risks and limitations are, however, typically less discussed than the potential benefits of PPPs, and can seem somewhat more abstract than the benefits. This is partly because, as discussed below, federal agencies currently rely upon various legal authorities in entering PPPs, and there can be some uncertainty as to whether particular PPPs are subject to specific legal requirements. Relatedly, there are fewer "real world" illustrations of these risks and limitations at the federal level, because federal agencies' use of PPPs for purposes of real property management has, to date, been fairly limited, particularly as compared to that of state and foreign governments.[31] Thus, this report generally discusses the potential risks and limitations of PPPs below, in the context of either the "Legal Framework as to PPPs" or "Considerations for Congress."

PPP STRUCTURES

PPPs can be structured in many ways, depending, in part, upon the legal authorities under which agencies enter and perform such agreements. However, despite this variability, PPPs—and particularly PPPs formed pursuant to agencies' authority to enter long-term leases of real property—generally share certain key elements. These elements, and examples of common PPP structures, are discussed below, as a way of illustrating the types of actions that agencies may wish to take in entering or performing a PPP and, thus, paving the way for a discussion of the "Legal Framework as to PPPs."

Key Elements of a PPP

The process of forming a PPP typically begins when an agency identifies a property that could provide greater benefits to the government if redeveloped or renovated. The agency then works with a nonfederal partner to determine whether a redevelopment strategy would provide the agency with the benefits it seeks, and the nonfederal partner with financial returns sufficient to cover the risk of investing in the property. If an agreement is reached, the partners typically enter into a master ground lease, which formally establishes the terms of the partnership, including (1) the length of the master ground lease; (2) the redevelopment strategy; and (3) the method of financing the redevelopment. Taken together, these three elements constitute the structure of a PPP. Typically, the master ground lease is a long-term lease of 50 years or more.

A long lease is preferable to nonfederal partners because it provides them with more time to recoup their investment and generate a profit. Generally, nonfederal partners seek a 15% return on their investment, sometimes referred to as the *internal rate of return* (IRR). If the market is not strong or the costs of the improvements are high—rendering a 15% IRR less likely—then the partner may want a lease that exceeds 50 years as one way to mitigate the increased risk.

The redevelopment strategy and the method of financing are closely linked. The former refers specifically to the work that the nonfederal partner agrees to undertake, while the latter is a combination of the revenue generated from the improved space and, in some cases, savings realized by reduced operating costs. A nonfederal partner might agree to renovate and modernize an aging VA medical center, for example, and, in return, obtain the right to construct and lease office space on the unused portion of the land. In this example, renovation and new construction are the redevelopment strategy; and the work is financed by revenue generated from leasing new office space on underutilized land.

Financial benefits to the government may also include a division of property cash flows. Under some PPPs, the nonfederal partner leases space from an agency, renovates that space, and subleases it at a rate higher than the rate it pays to the agency.

The rental payments the nonfederal partner receives are referred to as *operating income*. In order for the nonfederal partner to make a profit, however, the sublease must generate sufficient income to exceed not only the cost of the lease, but also operating costs and payments on debt incurred to finance the renovation. The amount that remains after deducting lease payments, operating costs, and repayment of debt from operating income is defined as the *property cash flow*. Typically, the nonfederal partner takes a "preferred return" from the property cash flow, then divides the remaining revenue—known as the *net cash flow*—into two shares, one of which the nonfederal partner keeps, and the other of which it pays to the agency. The government has two revenue streams in this scenario: (1) lease payments, and (2) net cash flow.

The amount that the government receives from net cash flows and the amount the nonfederal partner keeps are typically spelled out in the PPP agreement.

Examples of Common PPP Structures

There are many varieties of PPP structures, and the legal and policy ramifications of each are unique. However, several common redevelopment and financing structures can be identified.

- A federal agency holds underutilized land that includes four nearly vacant warehouses. The property is in a market where there is a strong demand for federal office space. The agency enters a PPP under which a developer leases the property and constructs a new office building on the unused portion of the land. The developer subleases the warehouses and the new office space, which is partially occupied by the lessor (i.e., the federal agency) and partially leased by other federal agencies.

- A federal agency owns a historic building that is unoccupied and in disrepair. The property is in a desirable location, and public and private entities are expected to be interested in acquiring space. A developer leases the property and renovates it in accordance with historic preservation requirements. The first floor is subleased by retailers, and the city government subleases the office space on the floors above.

- A federal agency owns land with a deteriorating office building and a small parking lot. The property is in a market where there is moderate to strong demand for private sector office space. The developer demolishes the existing building and constructs a larger, modern office building in its place, which is partially occupied by the lessor (i.e., the federal agency) and backfilled by businesses. The developer also replaces the parking lot with a garage that has space for tenants and for public parking.

- A federal agency holds family housing units that are in need of repair. The agency wishes to retain all of the units due to a shortage of space. The developer repairs the existing housing units and is able to add new units on underutilized land owned by the same agency.

- A federal agency's utility costs are well above average due to antiquated heating and cooling systems. A business installs new, more energy efficient equipment. In return, the business is repaid for the cost of the equipment and installation, and receives 50% of the energy savings.

- A federal agency wants to add an annex to a multi-use facility it owns. A developer builds the annex in exchange for several acres of excess property. The value of the excess land is roughly equal to the cost of constructing the annex.

In-Kind Benefits

While the benefits obtained by agencies in the above examples generally consist of lease payments from the developer and monetary savings through reduced utility costs and maintenance backlogs, agencies may also receive "in-kind" benefits.

As a rule, agencies are required to obtain "fair consideration"—generally equivalent to fair market value—in exchange for selling or leasing real property.[32]

However, agencies may accept non-monetary benefits as consideration when expressly authorized by statute to do so. In-kind consideration can include the provision of goods and services to the agency, or its personnel or clients. Examples of in-kind consideration are illustrated below.

- A federal agency wants new transitional housing for the clients it serves. A local government agrees to build the new housing units on vacant land the agency owns. The local government leases the land from the agency and uses part of the housing complex for its own homeless programs. As part of the agreement, the federal agency's clients get priority placement for housing.
- A federal agency needs renovated office space. A developer agrees to lease the building, renovate it, and sublease space back to the agency. As part of the agreement, agency personnel are allowed to use the child care center in the renovated building at reduced rates.
- A federal agency has unused space in a lightly utilized, deteriorating office building. It leases a majority of the space in the building and permits the lessee to offset its rent obligations by $1 million in exchange for building a water tower that could be used by all of the building's tenants.

LEGAL FRAMEWORK AS TO PPPS

While many PPPs share the same key elements, discussed above (see "Key Elements of a PPP"), there is considerable variation in the legal authorities under which federal agencies enter and perform PPPs. This is largely because federal law is generally silent as to PPPs, *per se*, particularly PPPs for purposes of improving or disposing of federal real property.[33] Absent a statute that generally authorizes the formation of PPPs, agencies seeking to enter such agreements rely upon their authority to take the specific actions necessary to form and perform the contemplated agreement (e.g., lease property for a specific period of time, receive consideration in-kind). However, because individual agencies have differing authority to take such actions, the nature of the PPPs they enter can vary. Relatedly, because agencies must rely on other authorities—such as their authority to enter certain long-term procurement contracts—in forming PPPs, it can sometimes be unclear whether particular legal requirements that generally pertain to agencies' exercise of these authorities apply to their PPPs.

Legal Authority to Enter PPPs

Unlike some state laws, federal law does not define the term *public-private partnership*,[34] or, with certain narrow exceptions,[35] authorize agencies to enter PPPs, *per se*.[36] Instead, those agencies that have, to date, entered agreements that could be characterized as PPPs have done so under their authority (1) to lease, otherwise convey, or permit the use of federal real property; and (2) to enter procurement contracts.

A lease can be seen as a type of contract, whereby the owner of a particular property grants another party the right to use the property for a certain period of time.[37] However, under federal law, a lease of real property is generally not a procurement contract. The Federal Acquisition Regulation (FAR) defines a *procurement contract* as a "mutually binding legal relationship obligating the seller to furnish the supplies or services (including construction) and the buyer to pay for them"; and *supplies*, to mean "all property except land or interests in land."[38] Thus, contracts whereby the federal government acquires leasehold interests in real property are excluded from the standard definition of *procurement contract*. Leases whereby the federal government disposes of interests in land are similarly excluded because they do not involve a "seller" furnishing supplies or services to the government.[39]

Authority to Lease or Otherwise Convey Real Property

Because the opportunity to acquire or use federal real property, and enjoy certain proceeds therefrom, is typically what motivates prospective partners to enter PPPs with the government, federal agencies have historically relied upon their authority to lease or otherwise convey real property under their jurisdiction or control when entering PPPs.[40] Many agencies have such authority, notwithstanding the fact that GSA is commonly described as the federal government's "landlord,"[41] and, as a rule, is responsible for the leasing and disposal of federal real property.[42] Congress has enacted a number of statutes that authorize specific agencies, acting on their own and without the involvement of GSA, to lease certain real property for particular purposes.[43] For example, DOD has authority to lease nonexcess real property under its control for five or more years in exchange for the maintenance, repair, or environmental restoration of the property or facilities.[44] This and other examples are described in **Table 1**. Commentators sometimes describe agencies that have statutory authority to enter such "long-term" leases as having enhanced use lease (EUL) authority.[45] However, a number of statutes grant agencies authority that is tantamount to EUL authority (i.e., authority to lease federal real property to public or private entities for a number of years in exchange for cash or in-kind consideration), but do not use the term "enhanced use lease."[46]

Relatedly, some agencies also have authority to convey federal real property by means other than leases, or to permit certain uses of such property, that they could potentially rely upon in entering public-private partnerships. For example, Section 111 of the National Historical Preservation Act (NHPA), as amended, authorizes federal agencies to

> lease an historic property owned by the agency to any person or organization, or exchange any property owned by the agency with comparable historic property, if the agency head determines that the lease or exchange will adequately insure the preservation of the historic property.[47]

Section 111 applies government-wide. However, some agencies have similar authority to exchange one real property for another,[48] or give away certain interests in real property.[49] Other agencies have authority to permit nonfederal entities to use their real property or facilities for a fee,[50] or subject to certain conditions. The President, for example, may permit nonfederal entities to construct and operate international bridges, and require that these entities provide facilities or services to federal agencies for free as a condition of their permit.[51]

Authority to Procure Goods or Services

Procurement contracts are generally not as well suited to the formation and performance of PPPs as leases, because procurement contracts typically have shorter durations than leases,[52] and generally contemplate the agency paying the contractor for maintaining or operating federal real property.[53] However, there are certain provisions of federal law which authorize "long-term" procurement contracts that provide for the contractor to finance performance and then share in any savings that the agency may realize as a result of the contractor's performance. Perhaps the best known of these is Section 801 of the National Energy Conservation Policy Act (NECPA) of 1978, as amended, which permits agencies to enter long-term contracts "solely for the purpose of achieving energy savings and benefits ancillary to that purpose."[54] Such energy savings performance contracts (ESPCs) may, "notwithstanding any other provision of law, be for a period not to exceed 25 years," and

> shall provide that the contractor shall incur costs of implementing energy savings measures, including at least the costs (if any) incurred in making energy audits, acquiring and installing equipment, and training personnel, in exchange for a share of any energy savings directly resulting from implementation of such measures during the term of the contract.[55]

In other words, Section 801 of NECPA contemplates third parties financing the costs of modifications to the infrastructure of federal buildings in exchange for a share in any savings in operating costs that may result from these modifications. Previously, federal agencies had similar authority to enter into "share-in-savings" contracts for information technology, which provided for the contractor to share in any savings acquired through "solutions" that it provided for improving the agency's mission-related or administrative processes, or accelerating the achievement of agency missions.[56] However, share-in-savings authority expired in 2005.[57]

Legal Requirements as to PPPs

Federal agencies' general practice of relying on various leasing authorities when forming PPPs can lead to questions regarding the legal requirements to which such partnerships may be subject. Some have wondered, for example, whether agencies must issue solicitations for proposed PPPs and whether partners are competitively selected;[58] as well as whether workers on partnership projects must be paid locally prevailing wages and fringe benefits under the Davis-Bacon and related Acts.[59] In some cases, the statute that authorizes the lease also answers some of these questions by imposing specific requirements upon agencies' use of its leasing or other authorities (e.g., competitive selection of vendors). As previously discussed, the FAR[60]—which people generally look to for the requirements pertaining to federal contracts— does not apply to leases of real property, because the FAR governs procurement contracts, and leases of real property are not procurement contracts.[61] However, some agencies have adopted regulations which impose requirements analogous to those of the FAR upon their own acquisitions of leasehold interests in real property. Also, some federal statutes implemented, in part, through the FAR could potentially be found to apply to PPPs on the grounds that a lease is a contract,[62] or on similar grounds. In yet other cases, federal law does not appear to provide any guidance on certain questions likely to arise in the context of PPPs (e.g., selection of projects), or on the use of specific terms that potential partners are likely to seek in any partnership agreement (e.g., non-compete provisions). Some states, in contrast, have comprehensive guidance that addresses these and other requirements as to the PPPs of state agencies or local governments.

This section discusses various legal requirements that can apply to PPPs, including requirements deriving from (1) the specific statutes authorizing leases of federal real property or other actions that agencies rely upon in forming PPPs; (2) agency regulations that could be similar to the FAR; and (3) generally applicable statutory provisions pertaining to "contracts" or "public works." The section also discusses situations where federal law appears to be silent on particular issues relevant to the formation of PPPs (e.g., selection of projects, non-compete agreements). It similarly surveys the range of requirements addressed in certain—arguably comprehensive—state laws regarding PPPs to illustrate the various provisions that could potentially be made regarding agencies' formation and performance of PPPs.

Statutes Authorizing Leases or Other Agency Actions

As previously noted, agencies frequently rely upon specific statutes authorizing them to lease or otherwise convey real property, enter energy savings performance contracts, or take other actions when entering and performing PPPs. There are a number of such statutes. Few of these statutes apply government-wide, and those that do often apply only to specific properties, or for specific purposes. For example, as previously noted, agencies may rely on the authority of Section 111 of the NHPA,[63] to lease historic property only in order to "adequately insure" its preservation. Similarly, agencies may enter long-term contracts under the authority of Section 801 of the NECPA, only "for the purpose of achieving energy savings" and ancillary benefits.[64]

Further, NECPA defines *energy savings* specifically to mean reductions in the cost of energy, water, or wastewater treatment in existing federally owned buildings or facilities as the result of specified actions (e.g., improvement, lease or purchase of operating equipment), among other things.[65]

More commonly leasing and other authorities pertain to individual agencies and, often, to specific properties and purposes, as the examples in **Table 1** illustrate.

Such agency-specific statutes may regulate certain aspects of any PPPs entered by the agency, most commonly (1) the duration of the agreement;[66] (2) the type[67] and amount[68] of consideration received by the agency; (3) the terms under which conveyances may be made to different types of partners (e.g., state and local governments as opposed to commercial entities);[69] and (4) the retention and use of any funds received by the agency as a result of the agreement.[70]

Other guidance sometimes appears in statutes—such as guidance regarding the selection of projects and partners,[71] the terms and conditions of agreements,[72] and whether agencies must notify Congress or the public of proposed or finalized agreements[73]—but with less frequency. Conversely, in some cases, statutes expressly authorize agencies to take certain actions vis-à-vis real property "notwithstanding any other provision of law,"[74] or on such terms and conditions as the agency may determine.[75]

Table 1. Tabular Comparison of Selected Leasing Authorities

	10 U.S.C. §2667	10 U.S.C. §2812	38 U.S.C. §2412	38 U.S.C. §§8161-8169
Agency	DOD	DOD	VA	VA
Properties	Non-excess real property under DOD's control that is not presently needed for public use	Military installations under DOD's jurisdiction	"Undeveloped land," or any "unused" or "underutilized" facilities, which are part of the National Cemetery Administration	Property under VA jurisdiction or control
Purposes	Maintenance, repair, or environmental restoration of the property or facilities	Development of troop housing or energy production facilities, utilities, child care centers, and certain other facilities	Maintenance, protection, or restoration of the property	Development, maintenance, and operation of "supportive housing"
Maximum lease term	5 years (or longer, if a longer period will promote the national defense or be in the public interest)	32 years	10 years	75 years
Considera tion	Cash or in-kind, in an amount that is not less than fair market value, as determined by the Secretary	Not directly addressed in statute[a]	Leases to public or nonprofit organizations may provide for in-kind consideration	VA may enter leases without receiving consideration; however, any consideration must be cash at "fair value" as determined by Secretary
Terms for different types of partners	Certain unique terms and conditions apply when community support facilities and services are involved	Not directly addressed in statute[a]	Certain unique conditions apply when the lessee is a public or nonprofit organization	Not directly addressed in statute[a]

	10 U.S.C. §2667	10 U.S.C. §2812	38 U.S.C. §2412	38 U.S.C. §§8161-8169
Retention and use of proceeds	Proceeds are generally deposited in a specific account in the Treasury, and are available, in such amounts as provided in appropriations acts, for specified purposes (e.g., construction)	Not directly addressed in statutea	Proceeds from lease of land or buildings under 38 U.S.C. §2412, and certain other funds, are deposited in a specified fund in the Treasury, and are available until expended for cover costs incurred for national cemetery operations	Funds received under an enhanced used lease remaining after the deduction of certain expenses pertaining to such leases are deposited in the VA Medical Care Collections Fund
Selection of partners	Lessees generally must be competitively selected (with narrow exceptions)	Not directly addressed in statutea	Not directly addressed in statutea	Secretary may select lessees using "such selection procedures as [he] considers appropriate"
Lease terms	Lease must generally permit the Secretary to revoke it at any time, and may grant the lessee first right to buy the property if the lease is revoked. Lease may not provide for a leaseback by the Secretary with an annual payment in excess of $500,000	Lease must provide that, at the end of the term, title to the facility shall vest in the United States, and include terms and conditions "necessary or desirable to protect [U.S.] interests." Lease must also condition obligation to pay upon availability of appropriations		Lease may not provide for any acquisition, contract, demonstration, exchange, grant, incentive, procurement, sale, other transaction authority, service agreement, use agreement, lease, or lease-back by VA or the federal government
Notice to Congress & public	Not directly addressed in statutea	Lease may not be entered until DOD submits a justification and economic analysis to Congress, and a certain period of time has passed	VA must give "appropriate" public notice of intention to enter lease in general circulation newspaper in community where lands or buildings are located	VA must conduct public hearing in community where the property is located before entering into lease, and notify

Table 1. (Continued)

	10 U.S.C. §2667	10 U.S.C. §2812	38 U.S.C. §2412	38 U.S.C. §§8161-8169
Other provisions	Interest of lessee may be taxed by State or local governments	n/a	n/a	Congress, among other things VA may not enter lease unless Office of Management & Budget certifies in writing that it complies with these requirements. Improvements & operations on land subject to taxation

Source: Congressional Research Service, based on various sources cited in Table 1.

[a] Other provisions of law, beyond those authorizing the lease or other conveyance, could potentially be found to apply. *See infra* "Applicability of Requirements Pertaining to "Contracts" or "Public Works"."

FAR Generally Inapplicable, but Regulations Could Impose FAR-Like Terms

The FAR is arguably the best known feature of federal contracting. Even those who know little else about federal contracting are generally aware that the FAR exists, imposes specific requirements on agencies, and prescribes "standard" terms for inclusion in certain contracts. The FAR provides specific—often detailed—guidance on a range of topics, from planning acquisitions and conducting market research for purposes of identifying potential suppliers, to tendering and acceptance of performance, to contract payments and close-out. For example, the FAR requires agencies to make information about proposed contract actions available on FedBizOpps (https://www.fbo.gov/),[76] and imposes limits upon agencies' ability to award contracts noncompetitively based on *unsolicited proposals* (which are particularly likely in the context of public-private partnerships).[77] The FAR also establishes the framework whereby agencies comply with the statutory requirement to "Buy American" when procuring supplies and construction services,[78] and prescribes the use of specific contract terms granting the government the right to terminate contracts for default or the government's convenience.[79] However, as previously discussed, because the FAR only governs the acquisition of supplies and services and defines *supplies* to exclude interests in real property, its applicability to many federal agency PPPs is limited.[80] Only where an agency relies on its authority to enter a procurement contract— such as an ESPC—in forming a PPP will the FAR typically apply.[81]

On the other hand, there could potentially be cases where the FAR itself does not apply, but the agency has imposed certain requirements like those provided for in the FAR upon itself through the promulgation of regulations, or as terms of its contracts. Perhaps the most notable example of this involves the regulations governing GSA's own acquisition of leasehold interests in real property.[82] These regulations could potentially come into play in certain PPP arrangements, and frequently require GSA to comply with the FAR, absent exceptional circumstances. For example, these regulations require GSA to include "provisions or clauses that are substantially the same as the FAR provisions and clauses" regarding contract disputes in its leases.[83] The regulations similarly require that GSA generally obtain "full and open competition" through the use of "competitive procedures" when awarding contracts to obtain leasehold interests in real property,[84] and that GSA contracting officers comply with the FAR when requiring oral presentations for acquisitions of leasehold interests.[85] It is important to note, however, that

GSA's regulations regarding the acquisition of leasehold interests in real property do not parallel the FAR in all ways, and other agencies may not have similar regulations regarding the acquisition or conveyance of leasehold interests in real property under their own governing statutes.

Applicability of Requirements Pertaining to "Contracts" or "Public Works"

In some cases, other statutes—beyond those that authorize the lease, conveyance, or other action that the federal agency took in entering the PPP—could impose certain requirements upon agencies' partnership activities. Often, these are statutes which are implemented, in part, through the FAR, but which could be construed as applicable outside the procurement context because they refer to "contracts" or "public works." How particular PPP projects are structured can also help determine the applicability of such requirements.[86]

For example, insofar as leases of real property are deemed to be contracts,[87] they could potentially be subject to a range of statutory requirements that pertain to contracts,[88] as illustrated by the GAO's 2012 decision in *The Argos Group*.[89] In this case, GAO relied upon Supreme Court and other precedents holding that leases are contracts for purposes of the Anti-Deficiency Act and the CDA[90] in finding that GSA is required to accord "price evaluation preferences"[91] to Historically Underutilized Business Zone (HUBZone) small businesses when acquiring leasehold interests in real property. GSA had argued that such preferences are required only in procurements of supplies and services (i.e., procurements subject to the FAR), and a lease of real property is not a procurement contract.[92] However, GAO rejected this argument on the grounds that the relevant provisions of the Small Business Act—which requires price evaluation and other preferences for HUBZone small businesses—"do[] not limit the type of contract to which they apply."[93] Rather, according to GAO, the Small Business Act "broadly applies to *all federal contracts* that involve full and open competition."[94]

Similar logic could potentially cause public-private partnerships to be found to be subject to certain statutory requirements pertaining to "public buildings" and "public works." For example, a 2013 decision by the U.S. Department of Labor's (DOL's) Administrative Review Board (ARB or Board) affirmed an earlier determination by the Administrator of DOL's Wage and Hour Division that the CityCenterDC project is subject to the Davis-Bacon Act's requirements as to the payment of prevailing wages and fringe benefits.[95] The Davis-Bacon Act applies, in part, to the "construction, alteration, and/or repair ... of public buildings and public works of the [federal] Government [and] the District of Columbia."[96] Both the developer and the District of Columbia asserted that the CityCenterDC project—which called for the construction of several types of buildings on land that had been variously conveyed by the city to the developer pursuant to special warranty deeds, 99-year ground leases, and 20-year licenses—is not a public building or work. In making this argument, the developer and the city noted, among other things, that the developer, not the city, contracted with the builders on this project; "no public funds" will be used to pay for construction; none of the buildings will be constructed for use or occupancy by the city; and the benefits the city would realize from the project are the same as those it realizes from purely private developments (e.g., employment opportunities for residents, increased tax base).[97] However, the ARB rejected these arguments, in part, because it viewed the project as falling within DOL's definition of a *public work* as "any building or work, the construction, prosecution, completion, or repair of which ... is carried on directly by authority of or with funds of a Federal agency [or the District of Columbia] to serve the interests of the general public."[98] In particular, the ARB found that the work was carried on under the city's authority because "the terms of the ground leases, the development agreements, and the Master Plan collectively provide the District with authority over what will be built and how it will be maintained during the lease terms."[99] It similarly found that the work "served the public interest," since it entailed "substantial and continuing economic gains to the District," including the construction of a park and central plaza for public use, employment opportunities for district residents, and "substantial revenues" for the District.[100] The Board further noted that, under the 99-year ground leases and other agreements, certain buildings were to become the District's property at the expiration of the lease, or at an earlier date, if the developer failed to meet specified conditions.[101]

As the case of CityCenterDC suggests, how particular PPPs are structured can also play a role in determining the legal requirements to which such partnerships are subject. With CityCenter, the ARB specifically noted the "public entanglement" in various aspects of the development in finding that the development constituted a public building or work for purposes of the Davis-Bacon Act (e.g., the city's authority to terminate the ground leases if the developer failed to meet certain conditions).[102] This suggests that the ARB could potentially have reached a different conclusion had the PPP been structured in such a way that the District did not have the same authority over what is built and how it is maintained during the course of the lease, or if the economic gains to the city had been less "substantial" or "continuing." The structure of the particular PPP in question played a similar role in a 2007 federal district court decision finding that housing units and other infrastructure constructed and maintained on Marine Corps land by a private developer are not subject to local taxation.[103] Here, the government had conveyed the housing units, along with the "income stream from military personnel renting those ... units" to the developer under a 50-year ground lease.[104] Two local governments asserted that this was tantamount to a sale, and thus transferred title to the developer and subjected the project to local taxation.[105] The court found otherwise, noting that the "level of control retained" by the United States under the project indicated that "the government still holds the land subject to its 'primary jurisdiction and control.'"[106] However, the court expressly indicated that the outcome could have been different had the government sectioned off a portion of the land, effectively severing it from the military installation, and the developer then put the property to non-military uses.[107]

No Relevant Provisions in Federal Law

In other cases, neither the statute that the agency relied upon in entering the PPP, nor other provisions of law, provide guidance on certain topics, including topics that are likely to be particularly relevant in the formation and performance of PPPs. One such topic is the selection of projects. The primary constraints upon agencies' determinations as to which supplies or services to procure, and which properties to acquire leasehold interests in, are arguably based in appropriations law. Agencies generally cannot obligate funds in excess or advance of an appropriation;[108] and appropriations may only be used for their designated purposes[109] to meet *bona fide* agency needs.[110] Because the totality of agencies' needs typically exceed their appropriations, their ultimate decisions as to what to procure or acquire by lease typically depend upon their conceptions of their missions and the public interest. The same logic would not necessarily apply in the case of PPPs, at least insofar as these projects rely solely upon private financing.[111] Because of this potential disconnect between agency missions and the interests of potential private partners,[112] some states have enacted legislation that requires agencies to consider potential PPPs within the context of their broader priorities, and prohibits them from giving special consideration to forming and performing partnerships just because they have private financing.[113] There do not appear to be any comparable provisions in federal law.

Another example involves "noncompete agreements," or provisions which bar the government from taking certain actions that could interfere with its partner's ability to obtain the contemplated return on its investment during the term of the partnership. Such agreements are not standard features of federal procurement contracts or leases of real property, although certain *requirements contracts* could potentially be found to have been breached if the agency were to hire another vendor to perform these requirements (or perform the requirements itself).[114] However, a number of commentators have called for the inclusion of non-compete agreements in at least some PPPs, particularly those where a developer builds a facility and then operates it, relying on the revenue generated from the facility's operations to pay off the costs of construction.[115] In such situations, developers are likely to want an agreement whereby the agency promises not to develop or operate other facilities whose existence could cut into the revenue that the developer receives from operating its facilities, and commentators sometimes point to PPPs that have "failed" because they lacked such agreements.[116]

In such situations, federal agencies are currently generally left to their own devices in determining whether to take particular actions (e.g., undertake particular PPPs, consent to non-compete agreements). They are also responsible for drafting any contractual terms on their own, without the benefit of "standard" contract clauses, such as those provided in the FAR.[117] As a result, there could potentially be wide variation between agencies in terms of their willingness to enter PPPs, and the terms of any partnerships that they might perform. This variability could potentially limit parties' willingness to commit to PPPs, as well as public acceptance of PPPs, as discussed below. See "Legal Uncertainties Could Deter Use of PPPs."

Comparison to State Law

Federal law's general lack of guidance regarding the legal requirements governing agencies' PPPs is in marked contrast to state law. As of May 2013, at least 27 states had statutes which not only define *public-private partnership* and expressly authorize state agencies or local governments to form PPPs, but also provide guidance regarding specific aspects of their use.[118] In some of these states, as **Table 2** illustrates, the guidance can arguably be characterized as "comprehensive," in that it (1) addresses the powers of the state agency and its partner in such agreements; (2) generally requires the completion of feasibility studies before a partnership is undertaken; (3) prescribes procedures for the competitive selection of partners; (4) provides certain protections for offerors (including those whose proposals are not selected); (5) calls for the inclusion of specific terms in any partnership agreements; (6) establishes a framework for setting any user-fees; and (7) provides for the termination or expiration of the agreement. In other states, the guidance is more limited, and addresses only some of these topics.[119]

Table 2. Sample Provisions in "Comprehensive" State PPP Statutes

Topic	Selected Provisions
Powers of agency	State agency may take certain actions in developing, financing, or operating PPPs, and may use revenues arising out of PPPs to develop, finance, or operate such partnerships, or "as otherwise considered appropriate by the department" (IND. CODE ANN. §8-15.7-3-1).
Powers of agency partner	Partner may develop, finance, and operate qualifying projects, and impose user fees in connection with the use of such projects (IND. CODE ANN. §§8-15.7-3-2 to 8-15.7-3-4). Operator may also own, lease, or acquire any property interest or other right in order to develop, finance, or operate qualifying projects (IND. CODE ANN. §8-15.7-3-3), as well as make any user classifications permitted in the PPP agreement, and enforce "reasonable rules" to the same extent that the agency may make and enforce rules with respect to similar projects (IND. CODE ANN. §8-15.7-3-4).
Facilitating participation	Agency required to establish a program to "facilitate participation" in qualifying projects by small, minority, Indiana, and women-owned businesses, as well as businesses treated as disadvantaged business enterprises under federal or state law (IND. CODE ANN. §8-15.7-3-5).
Feasibility studies	Agency generally must have preliminary feasibility studies and economic impact studies conducted by one or more firms internationally recognized in the preparation of such studies on any parts of the project consisting of tollways, and must conduct public hearings on these studies in the county seat of the county where the proposed project would be located (IND. CODE ANN. §8-15.7-3-5(b)(1)). Feasibility study must be based upon a public-private financial and delivery structure, and the economic impact study must, at minimum, include an analysis of impacts on employment and commercial and industrial development (IND. CODE ANN. §8-15.7-3-5(b)(2)). After the feasibility and economic impact studies are complete, agency must schedule another public hearing on the project in the county seat of any county that is an "affected jurisdiction" (IND. CODE ANN. §8-15.7-3-5(b)(3) & (4)). Thereafter, the studies must be submitted to certain legislative committees for review before commencement of the project (IND. CODE ANN. §8-15.7-3-5(b)(5)).

Topic	Selected Provisions
Competitive proposals	Agency may pursue a competitive proposal procedure using requests for qualifications (RFQs), or proceed directly to a request for proposals (RFPs) (IND. CODE ANN. §8-15.7-4-2(b)). Qualifications must be evaluated based on requirements and criteria set forth in the RFQ (IND. CODE ANN. §8-15.7-4-2(d)). If there is no RFQ, agency must provide public notice of the RFP, and submit a copy to the budget committee for review before its issuance (IND. CODE ANN. §8-15.7-4-2(f) & (g)). Agency must determine the evaluation criteria appropriate for each project, include these criteria in the RFP, and evaluate proposals based on the criteria (IND. CODE ANN. §8-15.7-4-2(h)-(i)). Agency must also hold public hearings on the preliminary selection of the operator and the terms of the proposed agreement (IND. CODE ANN. §8-15.7-4-2(l)).
Selection of offer	Agency's decision as to operator is to be submitted to the governor and budget committee for review, and once the governor accepts the agency's determination, the agency may execute the agreement (IND. CODE ANN. §8-15.7-4-3). Agency may also withdraw the RFQ or RFP, decline to make an award and interview offerors, among other things (IND. CODE ANN. §8-15.7-4-5).
Protections for offerors	Agency may pay stipulated amounts to unsuccessful offerors who submit responsive proposals in exchange for work product contained in that proposal (IND. CODE ANN. §8-15.7-4-4). Contents of proposals may not be disclosed during discussions or negotiations with potential offerors, and all records relating to such discussions or negotiations may be treated as confidential (IND. CODE ANN. §8-15.7-4-6).
Terms of the agreement	Agreement must require the completion of any obligatory environmental analysis; ownership by the state of the property on which the project is located; and an expedited method for resolving disputes (IND. CODE ANN. §8-15.7-5-1.5). Agreement must also incorporate the duties of the operator, and any other terms and conditions that would serve the public interest, and may include provisions for notice of default and cure rights (IND. CODE ANN. §8-15.7-5-4). Agreement may provide for the delivery of performance and payment bonds or other security; review of plans for development or operation; maintenance of public liability insurance policies or self-insurance; monitoring of the operator's maintenance practices; reimbursement to the agency for services it might provide; filing of appropriate financial statements and reports; compensation or payments to the operator or others for specified purposes (e.g., development fees); compensation or payment to the department in the form of concession or lease payments, etc.;

Table 2. (Continued)

Topic	Selected Provisions
	date and terms of the termination of the operator's authority and duties; reversion of the project to the department; and the department's rights and remedies if the operator defaults (IND. CODE ANN. §§8-15.7-5-1). Agreement may not provide that the state or department is responsible for any debt incurred by the operator in connection with the delivery of the project (Id).
User fees	Department may fix and revise amounts of user fees that the operator may charge (IND. CODE ANN. §8-15.7-5-2).
Financing of project	Agency may make grants or loans for development or operation of qualifying projects (IND. CODE ANN. §8-17.7-5-3). For purposes of financing qualifying projects, department may propose to use all or part of available revenues, enter into grant agreements, access any designated transportation trust funds, access any other funds available, and accept grants (IND. CODE ANN. §8-15.7-8-5). May also enter into agreements to take specified actions (e.g., issue bonds) (IND. CODE ANN. §8-15.7-8-6). Public funds may be aggregated with private funds (IND. CODE ANN. §8-15.7-8-7).
Distribution of payments	If agency receives any payment or compensation, it must be distributed to the "major moves" construction fund; the state highway fund; the alternative transportation construction fund; or the operator for debt reduction (IND. CODE ANN. §8-15.7-5-5).
Termination or expiration of agreement	Upon termination or expiration of agreement, department may take over the project and succeed to all rights, titles, and interests in it, and may take specified actions if it does so (e.g., impose, collect, retain, and use any user fees) (IND. CODE ANN. §8-15.7-5-6).
Standards for plans and specifications	Any plans and specifications developed under agreement must comply with department's standards for other projects of a similar nature, and any other applicable state or federal standards (IND. CODE ANN. §8-15.7-6-1).
Treatment as public works, and otherwise	Operator need not comply with certain provisions regarding state procurements and public works (IND. CODE ANN. §8-15.7-6-2). Projects are considered part of state highway system for purposes of maintenance and enforcement (IND. CODE ANN. §8-15.7-6-3).
Tax treatment	Operators or others purchasing tangible personal property for incorporation into or improvement of a structure constituting or becoming part of land included in a project are exempt from gross retail and use taxes (IND. CODE ANN. §8-15.7-7-2), but income received by a project operator is subject to taxation in same matter as other income (IND. CODE ANN. §8-15.7-7-3).

Topic	Selected Provisions
Resolution of claims	Department must establish an expedited method for resolving disputes between and among parties (IND. CODE ANN. §8-15.7-12-2).
Non-impairment	Department may not take any action under this chapter that would impair the partnership, nor may political subdivisions of the state (IND. CODE ANN. §§8-15.7-14-6, 8-15.7-15.1).

Source: Congressional Research Service, based on various sources cited in Table 2.

CONSIDERATIONS FOR CONGRESS

In considering whether to expand federal agencies' ability to enter PPPs, or overseeing the use of existing PPP authorities, Congress may want to pay particular attention to certain topics, such as (1) the limited information currently available regarding agencies' PPP authorities and their use thereof; (2) the degree to which legal uncertainties may deter agency use, or public acceptance, of PPPs; (3) agencies' capabilities to enter and perform PPPs; (4) whether agencies should be required to develop business plans for their partnership activities; (5) whether agencies should be required to notify Congress, or obtain its approval, when entering into PPPs; (6) agencies' ability to retain and use net proceeds from PPP agreements; and (7) the interplay between PPPs and the current disposal process. Other issues could potentially arise in specific contexts, depending upon the nature of the partnership and the authorities under which it is entered and performed. However, the foregoing seven issues would appear to be common regardless of the context.

Limited Information About PPP Authorities and Their Use

Currently, there does not appear to be any comprehensive source of information about the various PPP authorities of different landholding agencies. GAO has issued reports on particular types of real property authorities that may permit agencies to enter PPPs (e.g., enhanced use lease (EUL) authority),[120] and it has conducted in-depth analyses of PPP activities at particular agencies.[121] However, GAO does not appear to have conducted a comprehensive analysis of *all* agencies' PPP authorities and practices.

Absent a more comprehensive picture of agencies' PPP authorities, it is difficult to compare various agencies' authorities, or evaluate how particular authorities have been applied, and what effect they have on reducing excess and underutilized space. Information about existing PPP authorities could be particularly useful if paired with feedback from real property managers at landholding agencies. GAO's report on EULAs, for example, included comments from agency officials regarding the benefits and limitations of particular authorities, as well as opinions on what types of authorities they would like to have and how the ability to exercise such authorities would improve real property management. One agency told GAO auditors, for example, that "budget scorekeeping rules under OMB Circular A-11 limit [its] ability to maximize usage of its EUL authority."[122] Further information of this type could help Congress draft legislation which meets specific real property needs—as identified by practitioners—and whose application is not limited by unanticipated factors, such as budget scoring rules.

Legal Uncertainties Could Deter Use of PPPs

The lack of detailed legal requirements can have certain benefits, particularly where PPPs are concerned. Some have noted that such partnerships differ from "standard" procurement contracts in that they require the parties to work together much more closely to achieve shared goals.[123] Thus, it has been suggested, flexibility as to the terms and conditions of such agreements is optimal because the agency and its partner(s) can devise an instrument that is best tailored to meet their needs.[124]

On the other hand, an argument could be made that, insofar as lack of detailed legal requirements results in uncertainty about what requirements apply to particular projects, it may limit parties' willingness to commit to PPPs, as well as public acceptance of PPPs. Both government agencies and prospective partners may be less likely to enter PPP agreements if they perceive there to be significant uncertainties about their rights and responsibilities under these agreements.[125] Similarly, the public could remain skeptical of PPPs if the agreements are seen as being entered into or performed in ways that contradict public expectations about how government activities are to be conducted. For example, there is a widespread expectation that the government selects its business partners competitively and impartially, after advertising its needs. This expectation could potentially be thwarted if an agency enters a PPP based on an unsolicited proposal with an entity that happens to be politically well connected.[126]

Questions About Agency Capabilities to Enter and Perform PPPs

PPPs can be complicated arrangements, requiring knowledge of a range of disciplines: real property, architecture, civil engineering, procurement, and law, to name a few. An agency that lacks a staff with expertise in these disciplines may be at risk of entering into an agreement that does not represent the best value for the government, and of making costly mistakes when implementing the agreement. According to GAO, agency expertise is one of the five key factors in the successful implementation of PPPs. Specifically, GAO reported that the "agencies we reviewed also told us that they established organizational structures and acquired the necessary expertise to interact with private-sector partners to ensure effective partnership."[127]

The monetary consequences of poorly trained staff entering into real property contracts were illustrated in 2010 when the Securities and Exchange Commission (SEC) entered into a $556 million lease for 900,000 square feet of office space in Washington, DC—600,000 square feet more than the amount of space the agency needed.[128] Among the factors that contributed to this "misguided leasing decision" was the fact that the SEC had only established a leasing office in 2009, and did not put leasing policies into place until 2010.[129] The lack of a solid real property organization within an agency can lead to poor decision making and costly mistakes. Congress may wish to evaluate the internal structure of landholding agencies, to ensure that they have the requisite expertise, before providing them with PPP authority.

Potential Requirements to Develop Business Plans for PPPs

The likelihood of developing a PPP that results in maximum benefits to both partners may be enhanced by the use of business plans. The U.S. Postal Service (USPS) has developed and executed business plans as part of its PPP management process for years.[130] The business plans include information about the "division of risks and responsibilities between the Postal Service and its private-sector partner."[131] According to USPS officials, business plans are critical to the successful implementation of PPPs, in part due to the fact that they are drafted jointly with the private partner.[132] Based on USPS's experience, other agencies might benefit from being required to develop business plans prior to entering a PPP. At a minimum, the development of a business plan should help ensure that the agency and its nonfederal partner(s) engage in ongoing discussions about how to structure the agreement to the benefit of both partners. The process of developing business plans may also facilitate the sharing of market information and thereby improve decision-making as the agreement is being negotiated. In addition, business plans provide a road map for PPP implementation, which may help the partners meet milestones and, if made public or shared with Congress, could potentially facilitate oversight.

Potential Requirements As to Congressional Notice or Approval

One of the ways Congress maintains oversight of real property decisions that are made by GSA— which is one of the government's largest landholding agencies—is through the prospectus approval process. Congress has enacted legislation that purports to prohibit appropriations from being made for certain property management purposes unless the House Committee on Transportation and Infrastructure (T&I) and the Senate Committee on Environment and Public Works (EPW) have "adopted resolutions approving the purpose for which the appropriation is made."[133] GSA is further required, in order "[t]o secure consideration for [this] approval," to transmit to Congress a prospectus of the proposed facility that includes a brief description of the building to be constructed, altered, or acquired, or the space to be leased, among other things.[134] In addition, GSA's annual appropriations acts have frequently provided that "funds available to [GSA] shall not be available for expenses for any ... acquisition project for which a prospectus, if required by the Public Buildings Act of 1959, has not been approved."[135]

While these "requirements" are probably not legally binding,[136] GSA has historically complied with them on the grounds that "[t]he relationship between GSA and its authorizing committees is paramount."[137] Similar provisions could potentially also lead to compliance, as a matter of comity, in other contexts, and requiring agencies to seek authorization before entering into PPPs could provide Congress with an opportunity to monitor agency PPP activity and evaluate the soundness of proposed partnerships. Alternatively, agencies could be required to provide Congress with, at a minimum, advance notice of proposed PPPs, as some states require.[138]

Agencies' Authority to Retain and Use Net Proceeds

Real property disposals, such as leasing federal space to nonfederal partners, often generate sufficient revenue that agencies may realize positive net cash flow. Should Congress consider expanding PPP authorities, one issue that may arise is whether agencies should be permitted to retain net proceeds, and, if so, with what limitations. Federal agencies generally say that the authority to retain net proceeds from the disposal of real property—and to use those proceeds as they see fit—is a strong incentive to lease or sell unneeded space.[139]

While permitting agencies to retain net proceeds may result in an increased willingness to use PPPs, some stakeholders believe that congressional oversight may suffer if agencies have too much latitude. Congress has many options for addressing these concerns. PPP legislation could require agencies to deposit net proceeds in the general fund of the Treasury as miscellaneous receipts, or to reduce the debt. This would establish complete congressional control over net proceeds, but could remove the primary incentive some agencies have for entering into PPPs. Alternatively, legislation could require agencies to deposit net proceeds into a fund designated for agency real property activity, and specify whether withdrawals require congressional approval through an appropriation law.[140] Requiring re-appropriation of net proceeds would add an additional layer of oversight, but might deter some agencies from pursuing PPPs since they would have limited control over the funds. Yet another option would be authorize agencies to use net proceeds for any real property activity they deem appropriate, without requiring congressional approval—an option which would provide agencies with considerable autonomy—or permit them to expend net proceeds for any function that the agency is authorized to perform. As this last option provides the least direct oversight, Congress could potentially also require agencies to report on how they spend their net proceeds.

Clarifying Interplay between PPPs and Current Disposal Process

As discussed earlier in this report, the real property disposal process is prescribed by statute. Once a property has been declared as "excess," it enters the disposal process and the agency that controls it must follow the required steps unless it has specific statutory authority to bypass them. Congress may consider whether underutilized and vacant properties should be evaluated as candidates for PPPs prior to being declared excess. Doing so would essentially establish a screening process whereby unneeded space was first considered for a PPP, and only if deemed unsuitable would it enter the statutory disposal process. This might result in a larger number of underutilized and vacant properties being redeveloped, but it would also reduce the number of such properties that could be offered to other federal agencies, conveyed to serve a public purpose, or sold outright. PPP legislation may also provide agencies with specific authority to bypass statutory disposal requirements. Doing so may increase the amount of interest nonfederal entities take in PPP options, because such entities know that agencies can keep a property out of the disposal process, where it might be tied up for months. It may also be the case that systematically screening properties for PPP suitability and offering them for redevelopment and renovation might take just as long as the "standard" disposal process. In the absence of data on the length of time it takes to finalize a PPP and the financial benefits that accrue to the government as a result, it is not clear whether giving agencies special authorities to dispose of unneeded space through PPPs would yield greater returns than disposing of the same properties through the existing process.

CONCLUSION

Congressional interest in PPPs for purposes of federal real property management seems likely to persist—and may increase—given the constraints of the current real property disposal process and of the fiscal climate. A number of potential benefits of PPPs have been identified, and the common elements of such partnerships are widely recognized. The legal framework governing federal agencies' use of PPPs, in contrast, is less clear. Federal law does not define the term *public-private partnership*; nor, with certain narrow exceptions, does it authorize agencies to enter PPPs, *per se*. Instead, federal agencies have historically relied upon their authority to lease, otherwise convey, or permit the use of federal real property, or their authority to enter certain long-term procurement contracts, when forming PPPs. However, because individual agencies have different authority to lease real property or take other actions in forming PPPs, there is often considerable variability in the types of PPPs they may enter. In addition, there can also be uncertainty as to the legal requirements governing agencies' use of leasing and related authorities in the PPP context. In legislating to expand agencies' authority to enter PPPs, or in overseeing their use of existing PPP authorities, Congress may wish to consider, among other things, agencies' capabilities to enter and perform PPPs; whether agencies should be required to develop business plans for PPPs; and the relationship between PPPs and the current real property disposal process.

End Notes

[1] *See, e.g.*, Daniel B. Klein & John Majewski, Economy, Community, and Law: The Turnpike Movement in New York, 1797-1845, 26 *Law & Soc'y Rev.* 469 (1992).

[2] Federal Real Property Council, *FY2010 Federal Real Property Report: An Overview of the U.S. Federal Government's Real Property Assets*, September 2011, at pg. 6.

[3] 123 Stat. 3187.

[4] Consolidated Appropriations Act, P.L. 112-74, General Services Administration—Real Property Activities—Federal Buildings Fund—Limitations on Availability of Revenue, 125 Stat. 911 (Dec. 23, 2011).

[5] *See* 41 C.F.R. §102-71.20.

[6] The six building predominant use categories as defined by the Federal Real Property Council are laboratories, hospitals, office space, barracks, family housing, and warehouses.

[7] Federal Real Property Council, *FY2012 Federal Real Property Report: An Overview of the U.S. Federal Government's Real Property Assets*, September 2013, at pg. 11.

[8] U.S. Government Accountability Office, *High-Risk Series: Federal Real Property*, GAO-03-122, January 2003, at pg. 9.

[9] U.S. Government Accountability Office, *Federal Real Property: DHS Has Made Progress, But Additional Actions Are Needed to Address Real Property Management and Security Challenges*, GAO-07-658, June 2007, at pg. 30.

[10] U.S. Department of the Treasury, Office of the Secretary, "Treasury Budget Supports Obama Administration's Efforts to Strengthen Economic Growth, Make Government More Efficient," press release, February 13, 2012.

[11] *See* 40 U.S.C. §102(3) (defining *excess property* as "property under the control of a federal agency that the head of the agency determines is not required to meet the agency's needs or responsibilities").

[12] 41 C.F.R. §102-75.50.

[13] *FY2010 Federal Real Property Report, supra* note 2, at pg. 6.

[14] Federal Real Property Council, *FY2009 Federal Real Property Report: An Overview of the U.S. Federal Government's Real Property Assets*, September 2010, at pg. 12.

[15] U.S. Government Accountability Office, *Federal Real Property: High-Risk Designation Remains Due to Persistent Management Challenges*, GAO-13-422, February 2013, at pg. 9.

[16] Particular agencies may have express statutory authorization to dispose of particular properties without following the "standard" process. *See infra* "Authority to Lease or Otherwise Convey Real Property."

[17] 40 U.S.C. §§521-528.

[18] 40 U.S.C. §§541-559 *See also* 40 U.S.C. §102(10) (defining *surplus property* as any excess property that the Administrator determines is "not required to meet the needs or responsibilities of all federal agencies").

[19] *See, e.g.*, 40 U.S.C. §550 (disposal of real property for certain purposes).

[20] 40 U.S.C. §545.

[21] U.S. Government Accountability Office, *Federal Real Property: Progress Made in Reducing Unneeded Property but VA Needs Better Information to Make Further Reductions*, GAO-08-039, September 2008, at pg. 39. The screening process also has certain benefits, but these are outside the scope of this report.

[22] *Id.*

[23] U.S. Government Accountability Office, *Federal Real Property: Progress Made toward Addressing Problems, but Underlying Obstacles Continue to Hamper Reform*, GAO-07-349, April 2007, at pp. 40-41.

[24] U.S. Government Accountability Office, *High-Risk Series: Federal Real Property*, GAO-03-122, January 2003, at pg. 41.

[25] 16 U.S.C. §470.

[26] U.S. Government Accountability Office, *Federal Real Property: Progress Made toward Addressing Problems, but Underlying Obstacles Continue to Hamper Reform*, GAO-07-349, April 2007, at pp. 40-41.

[27] *Id.*, at pg. 16.

[28] For more information, see CRS Report R43247, *Disposal of Unneeded Federal Buildings: Legislative Proposals in the 113th Congress*, by Garrett Hatch.

[29] *Structures* include a range of properties, such as parking lots, bridges, utility systems, storage facilities, and harbors. For more information, see the Federal Real Property Council's FY2010 Federal Real Property Report, Appendix C, at http://www.gsa.gov/graphics /ogp/FY_2010_FRPP_Report_Final.pdf.

[30] U.S. Government Accountability Office, *Federal Real Property: Progress Made in Reducing Unneeded Property, but VA Needs Better Information to Make Further Reductions*, GAO-08-939, September 2008, at pg. 5.

[31] *See, e.g.*, Fernanda Kellner and Oliveira Palmero, Are Share-in-Savings Contracting and Public-Private Partnerships Capable of Challenging Traditional Public Procurement Processes? 38 *Pub. Contr. L.J.* 633 (2009) (comparing the legal frameworks for and use of PPPs by the Brazilian and U.S. governments); R. David Walker, Enabling the Privatizing of Toll Roads: A Public-Private Partnership Model for New Jersey, 6 *Rutgers J. L. & Pub. Pol'y* 623 (2009) (use of PPPs by states).

[32] *Consideration* refers to a performance or return promise that is the inducement to enter a contract, and a lease can be seen as a type of contract. *See infra* note 87 and accompanying text. A legally binding contract requires, among other things, consideration from both parties. Federal law generally requires that consideration for leases of federal real property be in cash. *See* 40 U.S.C. §1302 ("Except as otherwise specifically provided by law, the leasing of buildings and property of the Federal Government shall be for a money consideration only. The lease may not include any provision for the alteration, repair, or improvement of the buildings or property as a part of the consideration for the rent to be paid for the use and occupation of the buildings or property.").

[33] In a number of instances, federal law uses the term *public-private partnership* to refer to agreements that do not involve the federal government, or real property. *See, e.g.*, 20 U.S.C. §1153 (calling for federal grantees to "demonstrate substantial public and private support" for the operation of certain facilities by implementing public-private partnerships between state or local public entities and private entities); 22 U.S.C. §2151b (establishment and operation of public-private partnerships within certain countries affected by the HIV/AIDS pandemic).

[34] Maryland, for example, defines *public-private partnership* to mean a "sale or lease agreement ... under which ... [a] private entity assumes control of the operation or maintenance of an existing State facility; or ... constructs, reconstructs, finances, or operates a State facility or a facility for State use and will collect fees, charges, rents, or tolls for the use of the facility." MD. CODE ANN., TRANSP. §4-406(a)(5). Connecticut relies upon a similar definition that also requires the state's partner to fund a minimum percentage of the project's cost. *See* CONN. GEN. STAT. §4-255(a)(3).

[35] *See, e.g.*, Southeast Federal Center Public-Private Development Act of 2000, P.L. 106-407, 114 Stat. 1758 (Nov. 1, 2000) (authorizing the General Services Administration (GSA) to enter into leases, contracts, cooperative agreements, limited partnerships, joint ventures, trusts, limited liability company agreements, and other agreements to provide for the acquisition, construction, rehabilitation, operation, or use of a specific site within the District of Columbia).

[36] *See, e.g.*, ARIZ. REV. STAT. §41-2559(A) (stating that specified agencies "may enter into public-private partnership contracts); TENN. CODE ANN. §54-1-136(a) ("The department of transportation is authorized to undertake public-private partnerships with transportation fuel providers ... to install a network of refueling facilities, including storage tanks and fuel pumps, dedicated to dispensing biofuels, including, but not limited to, ethanol (E85) and biodiesel (B20).").

[37] *See infra* "Applicability of Requirements Pertaining to "Contracts" or "Public Works"."

[38] 48 C.F.R. §2.101.

[39] *See, e.g.*, Arcus Props., LLC, B-406189 (Mar. 7, 2012) (describing the transfer of certain federal real property to a nonfederal entity as a "non-FAR real estate transaction").

[40] The terms *convey* and *conveyance* are not defined for purposes of federal property management law. However, these terms are generally understood to encompass any transfer of ownership or interest in real property by a deed, lease, or mortgage. *Jurisdiction* and *control* are similarly undefined for purposes of federal property management law, but *jurisdiction* typically refers to the power or right to exercise authority, while *control* refers to power over something.

[41] *See, e.g.*, Gen. Servs. Admin., Getting Started Using GSA, *available at* http://www. gsa.gov/portal/content/104772?   utm_source=OCM&utm_medium=print-radio&utm_term=HDR_6_Help_new&utm_campaign=shortcuts (last accessed: Oct. 19, 2013) ("GSA is the government's landlord, providing office and other workspace services for the federal government.").

[42] *See, e.g.*, 40 U.S.C. §541 ("Except as otherwise provided in this subchapter, the Administrator of General Services shall supervise and direct the disposition of surplus property in accordance with this subtitle."); 40 U.S.C. §584 ("[T]he Administrator ... may assign or reassign space for any executive agency in any Federal Government-owned or leased building."); 40 U.S.C. §3302 ("Only the Administrator ... may construct a public building.").

[43] Such conveyances are generally not subject to the regulations governing the disposition of federal real property prescribed by GSA. *See* 41 C.F.R. §102-75.110 ("Transfers of real property must be made only under the authority of Title 40 of the United States Code, unless the independent authority granted to such agency specifically exempts the authority from the requirements of Title 40."). They are also generally not subject to GSA's regulations regarding its own acquisition of leasehold interests in real property. *See infra* note 82 and accompanying text.

[44] 10 U.S.C. §2667. *See supra* note 11 for the definition of *excess property*.

[45] *See, e.g.*, U.S. Government Accountability Office, *Federal Real Property: Authorities and Actions Regarding Enhanced Use Leases and Sale of Unneeded Real Property*, GAO-09-283R, February 2009; David S. Schuman, Space Act Agreements: A Practitioner's Guide, 34 *J. of Space Law* 277 (2008) (discussing NASA's "EUL authority").

[46] *See, e.g.*, 51 U.S.C. §20145 (authorizing NASA to lease any non-excess real property under its jurisdiction to any person or entity for an unspecified term, and to accept in-kind consideration for leases entered into for the purpose of developing renewable energy production facilities).

[47] P.L. 89-665, 80 Stat. 915 (Oct. 15, 1966) (codified, as amended, at 16 U.S.C. §§470 *et seq.*). *Historic property* means "any prehistoric or historic district, site, building, structure, or object included in, or eligible for inclusion on the National Register." 16 U.S.C. §470w(5).

[48] *See, e.g.*, 10 U.S.C. §18240 (authorizing the secretaries of military departments to acquire facilities needed to satisfy military requirements for a reserve component by exchanging an existing facility with an executive agency, the United States Postal Service, a State or local government, local authority, or private entity).

[49] *See, e.g.*, 38 U.S.C. §2404 (authorizing VA to convey to any state, or political subdivision thereof, in which a national cemetery is located, all right, title, and interest of the United States in and to any government-owned or -controlled approach road to such cemetery, provided certain conditions are met).

[50] *See, e.g.*, 51 U.S.C. §50504 (authorizing federal agencies to allow nonfederal entities to use their space-related facilities provided certain conditions are met (e.g., the facilities will be used to support commercial space activities)).

[51] 33 U.S.C. §§535-535*i*. *See also* Buffalo & Fort Erie Public Bridge Auth. v. United States, 106 Ct. Cl. 731, 744 (1946) (government permitted to use facilities associated with bridge for free for immigration inspections); Julián Aguilar, Dispute over Border Security Could Cause Delay for Bridge to Mexico, *New York Times*, Oct. 20, 2013, *available at* http://www.nytimes.com/2013/10/20/us/dispute-over-border-security- (permit calling for the bridge builder and operator to relocate certain machinery).

[52] The prototypical federal procurement contract is for one year's requirements of goods or services, but its term could potentially be extended for up to five years through the incorporation and exercise of options provided for in the contract. *See* 48 C.F.R. §17.103. However, agencies do have some authority to enter into multiyear procurement contracts— often of five years' duration—in certain circumstances. *See, e.g.*, 10 U.S.C. §§2306b-2306c (procurements of defense agencies); 41 U.S.C. §3903 (procurements of civilian agencies).

[53] *See, e.g.*, 48 C.F.R. §2.101 (defining *acquisition* to mean "the acquiring by contract *with appropriated funds* of supplies or services (including construction) by and for the use of the Federal Government") (emphasis added).

[54] P.L. 95-619, 92 Stat. 3206 (Nov. 9, 1978) (codified, as amended, in relevant part, at 42 U.S.C. §8287). *See infra* note 65 and accompanying text for the definition of *energy savings* for purposes of Section 801 of NECPA.

[55] 42 U.S.C. §8287(a)(1).

[56] 10 U.S.C. §2332 (procurements of defense agencies); E-Government Act of 2002, P.L. 107-347, tit. II, §210(b), 116 Stat. 2934 (Dec. 17, 2002) (procurements of civilian agencies).

[57] Agencies do not appear to have made extensive use of their authority to enter share-in-savings contracts. *See* U.S. Government Accountability Office, *Federal Contracting: Share-in-Savings Initiative Not Yet Tested*, GAO-05-736, July 2005, *available at* http://www.gao.gov/new.items/d05736.pdf (noting various reasons for agencies' non-use of this authority).

[58] *See, e.g.,* Parkridge 6 LLC v. U.S. Dep't of Trans., No. 1:09cv1312, 2010 U.S. Dist. LEXIS 34182 (E.D. Va. 2010) (plaintiffs alleging, among other things, that various government entities violated the Virginia Public-Private Partnership Act by "engineering a sole-source noncompetitive contract with a private entity" without requiring that entity to put up capital or share risks, and seeking to have the project rebid on a competitive basis).

[59] For more on the requirements of the Davis-Bacon Act, see *infra* notes 95 to 100 and accompanying text.

[60] For more information on the FAR, see generally CRS Report R42826, *The Federal Acquisition Regulation (FAR): Answers to Frequently Asked Questions,* by Kate M. Manuel et al.

[61] *See supra* note 38 and accompanying text.

[62] Whether the government is the lessor or the lessee of the property could potentially play a role in determining the applicability of particular requirements. *See, e.g.,* Res. Conservation Grp. LLC v. United States, 597 F.3d 1238 (Fed. Cir. 2010) (finding that certain requirements pertaining to contracts to acquire goods or services were inapplicable, because the Naval Academy sought to dispossess itself of an interest in real property, not acquire one, when it leased the land).

[63] 16 U.S.C. §470h-3.

[64] 42 U.S.C. §8287(a)(1).

[65] 42 U.S.C. §8287c(2). *See* Appeal of Honeywell Int'l, Inc., No. 57779, 2013-1 B.C.A. 35,380 (Aug. 7, 2013) (finding, among other things, that the challenged contractual arrangement was void because proceeds from the sale of renewable energy certificates do not constitute *energy savings* under this definition). For more on the *Honeywell* decision and the meaning of *energy savings* for purposes of Section 801 of NECPA, see CRS Legal Sidebar, *Contract Board Decision Could Change the Way That Federal Agencies Structure Energy Savings Performance Contracts,* by Brandon J. Murrill, *available at* http://www.crs.gov /legalsidebar/details.aspx?ProdId=739&source=FeatureTopic.

[66] *See, e.g.,* 10 U.S.C. §2667 (authorizing leases of non-excess real property for five or more years); 38 U.S.C. §§8161- 8169 (authorizing enhanced use leases of up to seventy-five years for purposes of "supportive housing").

[67] 51 U.S.C. §20145 (generally requiring that NASA receive cash consideration for leases of non-excess real property, but permitting it to accept in-kind consideration for leases for developing renewable energy production facilities).

[68] *Compare* 10 U.S.C. §2854a (consideration equivalent to the fair market value of the property) *with* 38 U.S.C. §8201 (leases "for such consideration and under such terms and conditions as [VA] deems appropriate").

[69] *See, e.g.,* 10 U.S.C. §18240 (exchanges of certain facilities under the control of military departments with other federal agencies, the United States Postal Service, or a State, local government, or local authority); 51 U.S.C. §50913 (encouraging the acquisition by state governments of launch or reentry property that is excess or otherwise not needed).

[70] *See, e.g.,* 38 U.S.C. §§8162-8163, 8165 (any funds remaining after the deduction of an amount sufficient to pay for expenses incurred in connection with the lease are to be deposited in a specified fund); 51 U.S.C. §20145 (NASA may use any cash consideration received to cover its full costs in connection with the lease).

[71] *See, e.g.,* 38 U.S.C. §316 (VA authorized to lease and lease-back real property for purposes of the relocation of regional offices and medical centers, but such authority may be used "at no more than seven locations").

[72] *See, e.g.,* 10 U.S.C. §2667 (lease entered into under this authority may give the lessee the first right to buy the property if the lease is revoked to allow the United States to sell the

property); 51 U.S.C. §30303 (authorizing the construction of facilities for use in tracking and data relay satellite services on government-owned lands, so long as the contract includes a provision whereby the government may acquire title to the facilities when the contract expires).

[73] *See, e.g.,* 38 U.S.C. §§8164-8165 (VA to notify congressional committees of its intent to dispose of property subject to an enhanced use lease not less than 45 days in advance, and publish a notice in the *Federal Register*).

[74] *See, e.g.,* 38 U.S.C. §316(b) (authorizing VA, notwithstanding any other provision of law, to lease, with or without compensation, for a period of up to 35 years, certain property under VA's jurisdiction).

[75] *See, e.g.,* 38 U.S.C. §8201 (authorizing leases "for such consideration and under such terms and conditions as [VA] deems appropriate").

[76] *See* 48 C.F.R. §5.201(a).

[77] *See generally* 48 C.F.R. Subpart 15.6. An *unsolicited proposal* is "a written proposal for a new or innovative idea that is submitted to an agency on the initiative of the offeror for the purpose of obtaining a contract with the Government, and that is not in response to a request for proposals." 48 C.F.R. §2.101.

[78] *See generally* 48 C.F.R. Subparts 25.1 and 25.2.

[79] *See generally* 48 C.F.R. Part 49.

[80] *See supra* note 38 and accompanying text.

[81] *See generally* 48 C.F.R. §23.205.

[82] *See generally* 48 C.F.R. Subpart 570.1. These regulations are part of the General Services Acquisition Regulation (GSAR) and thus apply only to GSA, and only in cases where GSA is the lessee. *See* 48 C.F.R. §501.101(a) ("The ... GSAR contains agency acquisition policies and practices, contract clauses, solicitation provisions, and forms that control the relationship between GSA and contractors and prospective contractors."); 48 C.F.R. §570.101. GSA also has regulations, codified in Title 41 of the *Code of Federal Regulations,* regarding the disposition of real property. However, these regulations generally do not apply to leases or other conveyances of real property authorized under specific statutes. *See generally* 41 C.F.R. § § 102-75.110 ("[T]he provisions of this section shall not apply to transfers of real property authorized to be made ... by any special statute that directs or requires an Executive agency to transfer or convey specifically described real property in accordance with the provisions of that statute.").

[83] 48 C.F.R. §570.701(a).

[84] *See* C.F.R. §570.104 ("Unless the contracting officer uses the simplified procedures in subpart 570.2, the competition requirements of FAR part 6 apply to acquisition of leasehold interests in real property.").

[85] *See* 48 C.F.R. §570.107 ("The contracting officer may require oral presentations for acquisitions of leasehold interests in real property. Follow the procedures in FAR 15.102.").

[86] The jurisdiction in which the project is performed could potentially also help to determine the outcome in such cases. For example, subcontractors on federal construction contracts cannot maintain *mechanic's liens*—which are legal devices commonly used to secure payment on private construction projects—against federal property because the government has not waived sovereign immunity as to such claims. *See, e.g.,* F.D. Rich Co. v. United States for Use of Indust. Lumber Co., 417 U.S. 116, 122 (1974) ("Ordinarily, a supplier of labor or materials on a private construction project can secure a mechanic's lien against the improved property under state law. But a lien cannot attach to Government property, ... so suppliers on Government projects are deprived of their usual security interest."). However,

courts in some jurisdictions have permitted subcontractors to maintain mechanic's liens against leasehold interests in federal property specifically. *See, e.g.,* J.J. Sweet Co., Inc. v. White Cty. Bridge Comm'n, 714 N.E.2d 219 (Ind. Ct. App. 1999) (lien attached to the leasehold despite the land being owned by the federal government); Basic Refractones, Inc. v. Bright, 298 P.2d 810, 815 (Nev. 1986) (same); Tropic Builders, Ltd., v. United States, 475 P.2d 362, 366 (Haw. 1970) (same). Others have not. *See, e.g.,* North Bay Constr., Inc. v. City of Petaluma, 49 Cal. Rptr. 3d 455 (Cal. Ct. App. 2006) (declining to distinguish between property owned by the city for "government purposes," and property used "for proprietary purposes"); Hempstead Resources Recovery Corp. v. Peter Salamandre & Sons, Inc., 428 N.Y.S. 2d 146 (N.Y. Spec. Term 1980) (mechanic's lien cannot be placed on a leasehold interest in public land being improved for use as a solid waste disposal system because encumbering the leasehold would encumber the land).

[87] *See, e.g.,* Appeal of Robert J. Di Domenico, GSBCA No. 5539, 80-1 B.C.A. 14,412 (Apr. 23, 1980) (noting that "[a]lthough leasehold interests have, over the years, developed some of the incidents of real property, such interests remain personal property except where statutes have modified the common law rule," and "the modern trend has been to consider leases as contracts rather than conveyances of real property").

[88] Such leases would not, however, generally be subject to requirements pertaining to agencies' contracts to acquire supplies or services if they involve the dispossession of real property. *See supra* note 62.

[89] The Argos Group, B-406040 (Jan. 24, 2012).

[90] *See, e.g.,* Leiter v. United States, 271 U.S. 204, 206-07 (1926) (Antideficiency Act); Forman v. United States, 767 F.2d 875, 879 n.4 (Fed. Cir. 1985) (Contract Disputes Act).

[91] For purposes of the HUBZone program, a price evaluation preference generally works as follows: the procuring agency adds a factor of 10% to all bids or offers (except those from HUBZone small business that have not waived the evaluation preference and otherwise successful bids or offers from other small businesses) in determining which bid or offer is the lowest price or represents "best value" for the government. *See* 48 C.F.R. §19.1307(b)(1)-(2).

[92] The Argos Group, B-406040 (Jan. 24, 2012), at 13.

[93] *Id.* at 9-10 (quoting, among other things, 15 U.S.C. §657a(b)(3)(B) ("[I]n any case in which *a contract* is to be awarded on the basis of full and open competition, the price offered by a qualified HUBZone small business concern shall be deemed as being lower than the price offered by another offeror (other than another small business concern), if the price offered by the qualified HUBZone small business concern is not more than 10 percent higher than the price offered by the otherwise lowest, responsive, and responsible offeror.") (emphasis added)).

[94] *Id.* at 10 (emphasis added).

[95] *See* Application of the Davis-Bacon Act to Construction of the CityCenterDC Project in the District of Columbia, ARB Case Nos. 11-074, 11-078, 11-082, *available at* http://www.oalj.dol.gov/PUBLIC/ARB/DECISIONS/ ARB_DECISIONS/DBA/11_074.DBAP.HTM.

[96] 40 U.S.C. §3142(a).

[97] The developer and city continued to maintain these arguments when appealing the administrative decision in federal court. *See* CCDC Office LLC v. U.S. Dep't of Labor (filed May 21, 2013, D.D.C.) (copy on file with the authors); District of Columbia v. U.S. Dep't of Labor (filed May 20, 2013, D.D.C.) (copy on file with the authors).

[98] Application of the Davis-Bacon Act to Construction of the CityCenterDC Project, *supra* note 95, at 12 (quoting 29 C.F.R. §5.2(k)).

[99] *Id.*

[100] *Id.* at 13-14.

[101] Id. at 3-4.

[102] *Id.* at 3.

[103] Atlantic Marine Corps Communities, LLC v. Onslow Cty., 497 F. Supp. 2d 743 (E.D. N.C. 2007).

[104] *Id.* at 748. The federal government retained title to the land, and the lease provided that title to the housing and related improvements would be transferred back to the government (or other owner of the land) upon the expiration or termination of the lease. *Id.*

[105] *Id.* at 756.

[106] *Id.* at 758. The finding of "jurisdiction and control" here is significant because the U.S. Constitution, in what is commonly referred to as the Enclave Clause, grants Congress the power "[t]o exercise exclusive Legislation in all cases whatsoever, over ... all Places purchased by the Consent of the Legislature of the State in which the Same shall be, for the Erection of Forts, Magazines, Arsenals, dock-Yards, and other needful Buildings." U.S. Const., art. I, §8, cl. 17.

[107] 497 F. Supp. 2d at 758. *Cf.* Baltimore Shipbuilding & Dry Dock Co. v. Baltimore, 195 U.S. 375 (1904) (company's fee interest subject to state taxation where the United States conveyed land to a private dock company with instructions to construct and maintain a dry dock and grant the United States free use, and the property was to revert to the United States if these conditions were not met); Palmer v. Barnett, 162 U.S. 399 (1896) (finding that exclusive federal jurisdiction over certain property which it had leased to a city had terminated, at least during the term of the lease, because the state had ceded jurisdiction to the federal government "for the use and purposes of a navy yard and navy hospital," and the federal government had leased a portion of the land to the city of Brooklyn "for market purposes").

[108] *See* 31 U.S.C. §1341(a).

[109] *See* 31 U.S.C. §1301(a) (prohibiting the use of appropriations for purposes other than those for which they were appropriated).

[110] *See, e.g.,* Funding for Air Force Cost Plus Fixed Fee Level of Effort Contract, B-277165 (Jan. 10, 2000) (fiscal year appropriation may be obligated only to meet a legitimate—or *bona fide*—need arising or, in some cases, continuing in the fiscal year for which the appropriation was made). This is commonly known as the "*bona fide* needs rule."

[111] In some cases, agencies have express authority to use appropriated funds in performing agreements that could be characterized as PPPs. For example, Section 801 of the National Energy Conservation Policy Act was amended in 2007 to authorize agencies to use appropriated funds to partially finance energy savings performance contracts. Energy Independence and Security Act of 2007, P.L. 110-140, §512, 121 Stat. 1658 (Dec. 19, 2007) (codified at 42 U.S.C. §8287c(2)(E)(i)-(ii)).

[112] *See, e.g.,* Ellen M. Erhardt, Caution Ahead: Changing Laws to Accommodate Public-Private Partnerships in Transportation, 42 *Val. U.L. Rev.* 905, 948-49 (2008) ("By allowing the private sector to enter an unsolicited bid, many projects may become potential PPPs which would otherwise not be considered."); Karen J. Hedlund & Nancy C. Smith, "SAFETEA-LU Promotes Private Investment in Transportation," Aug. 1, 2005, *available at* http://www.transportation1.org/aashtonew/docs/pabs.doc ("Solicited bids enable the responsible public entity to communicate its transportation project priorities. Unsolicited

proposals, by contrast, enable the private sector to propose projects that the public entity might not otherwise have considered.").

[113] *See, e.g.*, Cal. Ed. Code §81004(b)(1) ("If a community college requests state funding for an education building or education center constructed through a public-private partnership, funding for that facility shall not supersede community college facilities that have been previously prioritized by the board of governors and are awaiting state funding. These facilities shall be subject to the board of governors' annual prioritization process and shall not receive higher priority for state funding solely because the facilities are constructed through a public-private partnership.").

[114] *See, e.g.*, Torncello v. United States, 681 F.2d 756 (Fed. Cl. 1982) (agency obtaining goods or services from another vendor); Kalvar Corp. v. United States, 543 F.2d 1298 (Ct. Cl. 1976) (termination in bad faith so as to use an alternate source); Maya Transit Co., ASBCA 20186, 75-2 BCA 11,552 (1975) (agency's developing additional in-house capacity to perform certain work breached requirements contract which entitled the contractor to supply those goods or services "in excess of the quantities which the activity may itself furnish with its own capabilities"). A requirements contract is one "by which one party, the seller, agrees to satisfy all of the agency's requirements for services and/or items for a specified period of time." Aviation Specialists, Inc., DOTBCA 1967, 91-1 BCA 23,534 (Dec. 30, 1990).

[115] *See, e.g.*, Emilia Istrate and Robert Puentes, Moving Forward on Public Private Partnerships: U.S. and International Experience with PPP Units, Brookings-Rockefeller Project on State and Metropolitan Innovation, Dec. 2011, at 13, *available at* http://www.brookings.edu /~/media   08%20transportation%20istrate%20puentes/1208_ transportation_istrate_puentes.pdf (noting that the "existence of some type of non-compete clause is attractive to the private sector because it lowers the risk of competition from substitute assets," and reporting that only five states expressly prohibited the use of such clauses).

[116] *See, e.g.*, Christopher D. Carlson, Public-Private Partnerships in State and Local Highway Transportation Projects, *The Federal Lawyer*, Nov./Dec. 2008, at 34, 37 (noting that, after the State of Virginia improved a "competing" road ahead of schedule, the developer on the Dulles Greenway project defaulted on its payments in 1996; the project had to be refinanced in 1999; and the project generated only 35% of its projected revenue in its fifth year). *But see id.* (noting that, in the case of the California State Route 91 project, the state had to purchase the road from its private partner, at a cost of $81.9 million more than the cost of building the road, in order to make improvements to non-tolled lanes of the road).

[117] Because they have been reviewed by multiple people and used in various contexts, "standard" clauses may be better drafted than clauses specially drafted for inclusion in particular contracts. Some commentators have noted that well drafted contracts are essential for ensuring performance under PPPs, and that agency contracting personnel may be ill-prepared to oversee the formation and performance of PPPs. *See, e.g.*, Peter C. Halls, Issues for Designers, Contractors, and Suppliers to Public Private Partnership Projects, *30 Constr. Lawyer* 22 (2010); David W. Gaffey, Outsourcing Infrastructure: Expanding the Use of Public-Private Partnerships in the United States, 39 *Pub. Cont. L.i* 351 (2009/2010).

[118] *See generally* CRS Congressional Distribution Memorandum, *State Laws Regarding Public-Private Partnerships for Property Management*, by Kate M. Manuel, May 28, 2013 (copy available by request from the author).

[119] Other states having "comprehensive" type guidance include Arizona, California, Connecticut, Florida, Georgia, Illinois, Louisiana, Missouri, and Virginia. States with more limited

guidance, addressing only specific issues, include Alabama, Alaska, Arkansas, Massachusetts, Minnesota, New Hampshire, New Jersey, North Carolina, Oklahoma, South Carolina, Tennessee, Texas, Utah, Washington, and West Virginia. The relevant provisions of these and other states' laws can be found in CRS Congressional Distribution Memorandum, *State Laws Regarding Public-Private Partnerships for Property Management, supra* note 118.

[120] *See, e.g.*, U.S. Government Accountability Office, *Federal Real Property: Improved Cost Reporting Would Help Decision Makers Weigh the Benefits of Enhanced Use Leasing*, GAO-13-14, Dec. 9, 2012.

[121] U.S. Government Accountability Office, *Defense Infrastructure: The Enhanced Use Lease Program Requires Management Attention*, GAO-11-574, June 30, 2011; U.S. Government Accountability Office, *VA Real Property: VA Emphasizes Enhanced-Use Leases to Manage Its Real Property Portfolio*, GAO-09-776T, June 10, 2009; U.S. Government Accountability Office, *NASA: Enhanced Use Leasing Program Needs Additional Controls*, GAO-07- 306R, Mar. 1, 2007.

[122] U.S. Government Accountability Office, *Federal Real Property: Authorities and Actions Regarding Enhanced Use Leases and Sale of Unneeded Real Property*, GAO-09-283R, February 2009, at pg. 15. OMB Circular A-11guides the preparation and submittal of budget estimates.

[123] *See, e.g.*, Chem Sev., Inc. v. Envir. Monitoring Sys. Lab.—Cincinnati of the U.S. Envir. Protection Agency, 816 F. Supp. 328 (E.D. Pa. 1993) (characterizing one type of public-private partnership agreement—a cooperative research and development agreement (CRADA)—as "much more flexible and subtle" than a procurement contract because success with a CRADA depends upon shared goals and the parties' ability to work together with a high degree of trust toward those goals, while parties to a procurement contract often lack common interests and goals).

[124] *See, e.g.*, Avoiding the Pitfalls of Public Private Partnerships: Issues to be Aware of When Transferring Transportation Assets, 35 *Trans. L.J.* 25, 25-36 (2008) *See also* Panel Discussion: Public Oversight of Public/Private Partnerships, 25 *Fordham Urban L.J.* 1357, 1371 ("One person's oversight is another person's red tape.") (statement of Wayne Hawley, Deputy Counsel to the New York City Conflicts of Interest Board).

[125] *Cf.* David W. Gaffey, Outsourcing Infrastructure: Expanding the Use of Public-Private Partnerships in the United States, 39 *Pub. Cont. L.i* 351, 359 (2009/2010) ("[T]he expansion of PPPs is significantly hindered by lack of a clear and comprehensive regulatory framework governing the[ir] use."). The author here specifically notes the lack of comprehensive regulations for determining whether proposed partnerships are in the public interest, or how national or local interests might be affected by particular projects.

[126] *See, e.g.*, Eden Township Healthcare Dist. v. Sutter Health, 135 Cal. Rprt. 3d 802 (2011) (declining to void two contracts due to alleged conflicts of interests involving two health care district officials who had ties to the contractor); Ellen M. Erhardt, Caution Ahead: Changing Laws to Accommodate Public-Private Partnerships in Transportation, 42 *Val. U.L. Rev.* 905, 949 (2008) (noting the appearance of impropriety, and the possibility of misconduct, if "stringent" competition requirements are lacking).

[127] U.S. Government Accountability Office, *Public-Private Partnerships: Key Elements of Federal Building and Facility Partnerships*, GAO/T-GGD-99-81, April 29, 1999, at pg. 5. The other key elements were: (1) responding to a catalyst for changing agency real property management policies and practices; (2) having express statutory authority to enter into PPPs; (3) developing detailed business plans to assist in PPP decision-making (discussed

below, "Potential Requirements to Develop Business Plans for PPPs"); and (4) having stakeholder support.

[128] Securities and Exchange Commission, Office of Inspector General, *Improper Actions Relating to the Leasing of Office Space*, Case No. OIG-553, May 16, 2011, at pg. 3.

[129] *Id.*

[130] U.S. Government Accountability Office, *Public-Private Partnerships: Key Elements of Federal Building and Facility Partnerships*, GAO/T-GGD-99-81, April 29, 1999, at pg. 5.

[131] *Id.*

[132] *Id.*

[133] 40 U.S.C. §3307(a)(1)-(3)).

[134] 40 U.S.C. §3307(b)(1)-(7).

[135] *See, e.g.*, Consolidated Appropriations Act, 2010, P.L. 111-117, 123 Stat. 3189 (Dec. 16, 2009).

[136] There are two interrelated reasons for questioning whether prospectuses are required to be submitted or approved in all situations contemplated by the authorities cited in footnotes 141 through 143. First, absent a constitutional amendment, one Congress cannot bind future Congresses. *See, e.g.*, United States v. Winstar Corp., 518 U.S. 839, 872 (1996) ("[O]ne legislature may not bind the legislative authority of its successors."). Thus, although Section 7(a) of the Public Buildings Act purports to bar Congress from enacting appropriations for public building projects whose purposes have not been approved by the committees of jurisdiction, Congress can nonetheless enact measures that permit the construction, alteration, or lease of space whose purposes have not been so approved. Perhaps most commonly, Congress appropriates funds to GSA for the construction, alteration, or lease of space for which a prospectus has not been submitted or approved, an action which is generally taken to reflect Congress's intent to fund the project notwithstanding the provisions of Section 7(a). *See GSA, Public Building Services Leasing Desk Guide*, last revised Sept. 2, 2011, at 11-2 (expressing the view that GSA, "[a]s a matter of strict interpretation of fiscal law, ... may obligate funds ... regardless of whether the Committees have adopted resolutions approving the project"). GSA then uses this appropriation, in conjunction with its statutory authority to acquire real property under the Federal Property and Administrative Services Act (FPASA), to undertake the project. Second, and relatedly, in situations where an appropriation has been made, GSA takes the view that the language in its appropriations acts barring it from using funds for projects for which prospectuses have not been approved constitutes a "legislative veto that violates the separation of powers provisions of the U.S. Constitution." *Id.* The term *legislative veto* is commonly used to describe a provision that authorizes one House (or committee) of Congress, acting alone, to invalidate an executive branch action. In *Immigration and Naturalization Service v. Chadha*, the Supreme Court found that legislative vetoes violate the constitutional requirement that legislative acts be passed by both houses of Congress and presented for the President's approval. 462 U.S. 919 (1983). GSA asserts, arguably correctly, that a provision that effectively permits one committee of Congress to disapprove (by declining to adopt a resolution of approval) a project the executive branch is undertaking pursuant to authority delegated to it by Congress (through FPASA and an appropriation) constitutes a legislative veto.

[137] GSA, *Public Building Services Leasing Desk Guide*, last revised Sept. 2, 2011, at 11-2 ("The Committees expect that GSA will not award any projects over the threshold unless approved, and, as a matter of comity, GSA honors that expectation. GSA's policy is not to

enter into [projects] above the prospectus threshold unless the Committees adopt resolutions approving the project.").

[138] *See, e.g.*, IND. CODE ANN. §8-15.7-3-5(b)(5).

[139] U.S. Government Accountability Office, *Federal Real Property: Authorities and Actions Regarding Enhanced Use Leases and Sale of Unneeded Real Property*, GAO-09-283R, February 2009, at pg. 4.

[140] *See, e.g.*, 10 U.S.C. §2607 (proceeds from the sale of certain property received as a gift shall be deposited in the Treasury and be available for disbursement to the extent provided in annual appropriation acts).

In: Federal Real Property Management ISBN: 978-1-63321-219-0
Editor: Aaron F. Darby © 2014 Nova Science Publishers, Inc.

Chapter 2

FEDERAL REAL PROPERTY: STRATEGIC PARTNERSHIPS AND LOCAL COORDINATION COULD HELP AGENCIES BETTER UTILIZE SPACE[*]

United States Government Accountability Office

WHY GAO DID THIS STUDY

GAO designated the federal government's management of its nearly 400,000 real property assets as high-risk in part because of overreliance on leasing and the retention of excess facilities. Real property management is coordinated nationally by the FRPC—an association of landholding agencies chaired by the Deputy Director for Management of the Office of Management and Budget (OMB). To explore the potential to reduce leasing by better utilizing owned properties, GAO was asked to examine: (1) the potential for collocation and the factors that can affect that potential, (2) the possible benefits of collocation, and (3) the challenges associated with collocation, and what solutions, if any, can mitigate these challenges. GAO reviewed property data and documents from eight of the largest property-holding agencies; laws, regulations and guidance; and prior GAO reports. GAO also analyzed eight

---

[*] This is an edited, reformatted and augmented version of United States Government Accountability Office publication, No. GAO-12-779, dated July 2012.

case study markets of varying size and federal agency presence, and interviewed agency officials.

WHAT GAO RECOMMENDS

OMB should work with FRPC and USPS to, among other things, (1) lead the creation of strategic partnerships between GSA and other property-owning federal agencies with less experience sharing real property, and (2) establish a mechanism (including USPS) for local coordination to improve coordination and identify specific opportunities to share space. OMB, GSA, and USPS generally agreed with the recommendations. The details of agencies' comments and GAO's response are addressed more fully within the report.

Recently renovated space.

World War II era storage hut in present day.

Source: GAO.

Figure. Condition of Federally Owned Property with Underutilized Space.

WHAT GAO FOUND

The federal government owns facilities that are underutilized in locations where it also leases space. In some cases, space within these government-owned properties could be occupied by other government agencies. This is particularly true for the U.S. Postal Service (USPS), for which declining mail volume and operational changes have freed space in many facilities. However, this potential for collocation of federal agencies is affected by such factors as the size, location, and condition of the available space (see figure).

Officials from various agencies said that, in some cases, collocation could result in more efficient service delivery and cost savings or avoidance. For example, underutilized USPS floor and retail window space could be used by other federal agencies, generating space-use efficiencies for USPS and expanding citizen access to government services. Collocation could also help achieve agency synergies, such as shared technology infrastructure.

Agency officials said that strategic partnerships among federal agencies targeted to meet specific needs and a formal local coordination mechanism could mitigate certain challenges to collocation, including administrative and data challenges. Agencies have varying authorities to share available space in their properties and differing capabilities to handle the administrative tasks associated with sharing space. The General Services Administration (GSA), as the federal government's property manager, possesses the capability and experience to market properties and manage leases on a large scale. Officials from other agencies suggested that partnerships with GSA or a private entity could address some administrative challenges and improve collocation efforts. However, the ability to identify collocation opportunities is hindered by the lack of a formal information-sharing mechanism. The Federal Real Property Council (FRPC) is a national, policy-oriented body and, as such, does not manage the local-level negotiations that collocation would require. The FRPC established a database describing all executive branch properties, but it was not designed to identify and manage collocation opportunities, nor does it include USPS data. In contrast, local federal officials indicated that they possess detailed knowledge of specific properties owned by their respective agencies and, with more structured local coordination, could share that knowledge to support collocation efforts. GSA officials said that local councils were an effective method for sharing information.

ABBREVIATIONS

CPRA	Civilian Property Realignment Act
DEA	Drug Enforcement Administration
DHS	Department of Homeland Security
DOD	Department of Defense
DOE	Department of Energy
FBF	Federal Buildings Fund
FBI	Federal Bureau of Investigation
FRPC	Federal Real Property Council
FRPP	Federal Real Property Profile
FSA	Farm Service Agency
GPRA	Government Performance and Results Act
GRPIS	Governmentwide Real Property Information Sharing program
GSA	General Services Administration
IG	Inspector General
IRS	Internal Revenue Service
NRCS	Natural Resources Conservation Service
NPS	National Park System
OIG	Office of Inspector General
OMB	Office of Management and Budget
SSA	Social Security Administration
UFC	Unified Facilities Criteria
USDA	Department of Agriculture
USPS	U. S. Postal Service
VA	Department of Veterans Affairs

July 25, 2012

The Honorable Thomas R. Carper
Chairman
Subcommittee on Federal Financial Management
Government Information, Federal Services,
and International Security
Committee on Homeland Security
and Governmental Affairs
United States Senate

Dear Mr. Chairman:

The federal government's real property inventory includes nearly 400,000 owned and leased buildings located throughout the country.[1] As we have reported, the federal government retains more owned property than it needs while simultaneously leasing property from other entities, a practice that is not cost-efficient in the long run, resulting in millions of dollars of additional costs to the federal government.[2] In addition to an overreliance on leasing, federal agencies continue to face long-standing problems, such as excess and underutilized property and protecting federal facilities. Because of these issues, we have designated the management of federal real property as a high-risk area.[3]

There are current efforts promoting colocation—moving federal operations from one stand-alone location to a federal location occupied by another entity—and real property management reform. For example, several versions of the Civilian Property Realignment Act (CPRA) are pending in Congress and are aimed at, among other things, reducing the operating and maintenance costs of federal civilian real properties by disposing of unneeded properties; realigning other properties by consolidating, colocating, and reconfiguring space; and by realizing other operational efficiencies.[4] A Senate bill, the Federal Real Property Asset Management Reform Act of 2012, would 1) impose new duties on federal agencies to maintain inventory controls and establish goals for reducing inventories of underutilized properties, 2) establish and direct the Federal Real Property Council (FRPC)—chaired by the Office of Management and Budget (OMB)—to establish an asset management plan and submit an asset disposal plan, and 3) require the Administrator of General Services Administration (GSA) and the FRPC to establish and maintain a database of agency real property.[5] Additionally, postal reform legislation includes a specific provision related to colocation between USPS and other federal agencies, establishing and tasking the FRPC with identifying federal agency field offices that could be colocated with USPS and other civilian properties and permitting federal agencies to lease space for their field offices from USPS.[6] In May 2012, OMB also released a memorandum directing agencies to offset any growth in new building space with corresponding decreases through consolidations, colocations, or disposal of space from the agency's inventory.[7]

To help inform the discussion, you asked us to examine issues surrounding opportunities for colocating federal agencies by which the federal government could reduce privately owned, leased space by consolidating onto underutilized federally owned property. This report addresses:

1. whether the potential for colocation exists and, if so, what factors can affect that potential;
2. the potential benefits of colocation; and
3. the challenges associated with colocation and what solutions, if any, might help mitigate these challenges.

To examine these issues, we analyzed real property data from eight agencies with substantial domestic property portfolios: the Departments of Agriculture (USDA), Defense (DOD), Energy (DOE), Homeland Security (DHS), Interior (Interior), and Veterans Affairs (VA); GSA; and the U. S. Postal Service (USPS). Using available real property data provided by the agencies and ranging from fiscal years 2007 to 2012, supplemented by interviews with regional and national level agency officials, we selected eight U.S. markets in which we conducted case studies. We selected these eight markets to represent markets of various sizes, geographic regions, owned and leased federal properties, and agencies present. In the case study markets with DOD properties, we focused only on DOD properties not located on military bases. We also reviewed relevant legislation and analyzed data and documentation provided by the agencies.

We conducted this performance audit from July 2011 through July 2012 in accordance with generally accepted government-auditing standards. Those standards require that we plan and perform the audit to obtain sufficient, appropriate evidence to provide a reasonable basis for our findings and conclusions based on our audit objectives. We believe that the evidence obtained provides a reasonable basis for our findings and conclusions based on our audit objectives. Further details on our scope and methodology can be found in appendix I.

BACKGROUND

Federal Real Property

The federal government's vast real property inventory reflects the diversity of agencies' missions and includes office buildings, prisons, post offices, courthouses, laboratories, and border stations. The Federal Real

Property Profile (FRPP) is a database of owned and leased space held by executive branch agencies. It is maintained by GSA on behalf of the FRPC, although FRPC controls access to the data.[8] In 2010, FRPP data indicated that 24 executive branch agencies held about 3.35-billion square feet of building space.[9] These agencies reported that 79 percent of the total reported building space was federal-government owned; 17 percent was leased, and 4 percent of the space was otherwise managed.[10] The eight agencies we reviewed—USDA, DOD, DOE, DHS, DOI, VA, GSA, and USPS—reported holding over 3.32-billion square feet of building space or about 99 percent of reported square footage.

Owned and Leased Space

GSA and USPS are the largest civilian holders of federally owned property. They hold the largest amounts of space, by square foot, of the civilian agencies that we examined. As noted previously, we excluded much of DOD's property from the scope of our review because of the security requirements of traditional military bases, which would make colocation with other agencies unlikely. GSA and USPS together hold more square footage— almost 660-million square feet—than the other agencies we reviewed, excluding DOD, combined—over 454-million square feet. (See fig. 1.)

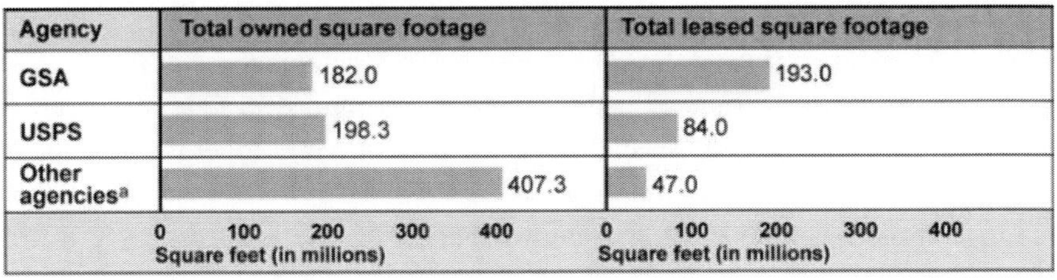

Agency	Total owned square footage	Total leased square footage
GSA	182.0	193.0
USPS	198.3	84.0
Other agencies[a]	407.3	47.0
	0 100 200 300 400 Square feet (in millions)	0 100 200 300 400 Square feet (in millions)

Sources: GAO analysis of GSA, DHS, USPS, and FRPP data.

[a] DOD data are excluded from this analysis.

Note: This analysis includes active buildings only; land and structures or property that are disposed, excess, or inactive are not included. USDA, DOE, GSA-"leased," Interior, VA data are from fiscal year 2010; DHS and GSA-"owned" data are from fiscal year 2011, and USPS data are from fiscal year 2012.

Figure 1. Total Square Footage Comparison for Federal Civilian Agencies' Properties, Fiscal Years 2010 to 2012.

Additionally, both agencies have a wide national presence—GSA-held properties exist in over 750 markets and USPSheld property is in almost 36,000 cities and towns.

Federal agencies, particularly GSA in its role as broker and property manager to the civilian portion of the U.S. government, rely on costly leasing, and the number of federal government leases has increased in recent years. The civilian federal agencies we reviewed held leases in close to 41,000 assets covering nearly 324-million square feet of space, with GSA and USPS leasing the most space.[11] Nearly all of GSA's leases are for other tenant agencies—for example, its four largest customers in the leased inventory are the Department of Justice, DHS, the Social Security Administration (SSA), and Department of Treasury (Treasury)— based upon those agencies' identified needs. According to GSA's annual portfolio report, since fiscal year 2008, its leased inventory has experienced faster growth than its owned inventory. We have reported that over time GSA has relied heavily on operating leases to meet new long-term needs because it lacks up-front funding needed to purchase buildings or space.[12] In addition, GSA has reported operational losses related to leasing, once indirect overhead expenses have been allocated, in recent years.[13,14]

GSA's Role

GSA is authorized by law to acquire, manage, utilize, and dispose of real property for most federal agencies. GSA is able to enter into lease agreements for up to 20 years that the Administrator of GSA considers to be in the interest of the federal government and necessary to accommodate a federal agency.[15] GSA uses this authority to lease space on behalf of many federal government agencies.

In 2004, the administration added managing federal real property to the President's Management Agenda and the President issued an executive order, applicable to 24 executive departments and agencies 1) establishing FRPC and 2) requiring FRPC to work with GSA to establish and maintain a single, comprehensive database describing the nature, use, and extent of all federal real property held by executive branch agencies, except when otherwise required for reasons of national security. [16] FRPC worked with GSA to create the FRPP to meet this requirement. FRPC is chaired by the Deputy Director for Management of OMB and is composed of Senior Real Property Officers from the 24 executive departments and agencies, the Controller of OMB, the Administrator of GSA, and any other full-time or permanent part-time federal officials or employees as deemed necessary by the Chairman of the Council. The order does not apply to USPS and FRPC does not work directly with USPS on the management of its real property.[17] These efforts notwithstanding, we have previously reported that the federal government continues to face a number of challenges to effectively managing its real property.[18] In particular, we have reported on challenges to disposing of excess properties, making better use of properties that are underutilized, and reducing overreliance on leasing.[19]

USPS Challenges

USPS, which is an independent establishment of the executive branch, is authorized to sell, lease, or dispose of property and is exempt from most federal laws dealing with real property and contracting.[20] Although declining mail volume and changes to its operations have resulted in excess capacity and facility space throughout the postal network, our recent work has shown that USPS faces challenges, such as legal restrictions and local stakeholder influences, that have limited its ability to close postal facilities in order to restructure its retail and processing network.[21] For example, USPS has often faced resistance from affected employees, communities, and elected officials when it has attempted to consolidate its processing operations and networks or close mail-processing facilities because of concerns about possible effects on service, employees, and communities. USPS recently announced that it will maintain existing retail locations, with modified operating hours. As a result of these issues, USPS has more space than it needs. Our recent work has also shown that USPS faces a deteriorating financial condition. For example, at the end of fiscal year 2011, the USPS had incurred a $5.1-billion loss for the year, had $2 billion remaining on its $15-billion borrowing limit,[22] and projects it will be unable to make its $5.5 billion scheduled retiree health benefits payment to the federal government.[23] In addition, USPS was conceived as a financially self-sufficient entity, but its revenues do not cover costs at about 80 percent of its retail facilities.[24]

UNDERUTILIZED OWNED FEDERAL SPACE EXISTS, BUT SIZE, LOCATION, AND CONDITION AFFECT COLOCATION POTENTIAL

Underutilized Owned Space

The federal government owns facilities that are underutilized in locations where it also leases space for different purposes. This is particularly true for USPS, as declining mail volume and changes in operations have freed space in many owned facilities. While there are problems with using governmentwide data to identify underutilized space, as will be discussed later in this report, we observed underutilized space held by multiple federal entities in the case study markets we visited for this report. For example, in each case study market, we observed one or more cases of vacant or underutilized space in post offices, including both offices and space on the processing floor, that officials said could be re-configured and physically separated from USPS operations (see fig. 2.)

Vacant USPS offices (top) and underutilized spaces on the processing floor (bottom).
Source: GAO.

Figure 2. Examples of Vacant and Underutilized USPS Space.

In some cases, spaces within these underutilized owned properties could be used by other government agencies. According to a recent report by the USPS Office of Inspector General (OIG) related to post office utilization, excess floor and retail window space exists nationwide that could be used by other government agencies or used to perform transactions on behalf of other government agencies.[25] The USPS OIG's office also conducted several regional studies examining excess USPS space and noted a correlation between space leased by GSA and the ability of USPS to significantly accommodate federal space needs. For example, one of those studies estimated that of the USPS districts reviewed, USPS excess space may accommodate 147 of 175 (or 84 percent) of agencies' current federal leases, and noted that GSA paid considerably more per square foot than the value assigned to USPS space. However, the Inspector General (IG) did not determine whether the excess space identified was usable for sharing with other agencies, in part because USPS systems and policies do not identify usable areas, and noted that more information would be necessary to determine whether USPS's excess space would be suitable for another government tenant.

Space Size, Location, and Condition Affect Colocation Potential

We observed several attributes that could affect using underutilized space for colocation. These attributes included size, location, and condition, which would likely render some spaces more appropriate for sharing than others. Much of the underutilized space we observed was small—only several hundred to a few thousand square feet. We also observed underutilized space that was not contiguous. Both of these attributes could limit those spaces' suitability for effective colocation. Furthermore, underutilized space that we observed varied in terms of its location within facilities. For example, GSA and VA officials described having some space that is less desirable to potential tenants. Although we observed generally high occupancy in GSA's multi-agency federal buildings, GSA officials showed us some space they said is not easily leased because of its location, such as a first floor interior office bordering the building's maintenance hallways or windowless basement spaces, and noted that these extra spaces can remain in GSA buildings when an agency does not require the entirety of a vacant space. VA officials noted similar issues, in that empty or available space at its campuses is often located in buildings surrounded by other VA buildings, which can make it harder for outside parties to access and use.

Additionally, we observed underutilized space in a wide range of conditions, from rundown to newly renovated, which could also affect colocation options. GSA officials said that a variety of physical aspects of the space may factor into the desirability of the space for colocation, including ceiling height, support column size, lighting, and windows. For example, Figure 3 shows interior office space in a GSA-held federal building in downtown Dallas that GSA officials told us has been vacant for years, a vacancy that they attributed to the lack of natural light and the large support columns that make it difficult to place workstations.

Source: GAO.

Figure 3. GSA-Held Vacant Space in Dallas, Texas.

COLOCATION COULD YIELD SERVICE-DELIVERY EFFICIENCY AND COST- AVOIDANCE BENEFITS IN SOME CASES

Federal officials we spoke with indicated that colocation could result in improved government operations through increased efficiencies for service access or delivery to the public in some cases. For example, VA officials stated that their incentive for colocation is to expand veterans' medical care efficiently, and that sharing space with other agencies with similar missions, such as the U.S. Army, could help achieve that goal and avoid duplicating medical capacity. Moreover, according to a recent report by the USPS OIG, the Postal Service would benefit from sharing post office space with other government entities while generating revenue and increasing efficiency by expanding citizen access to government operations. For example, USPS currently has interagency agreements to provide non-postal government services, such as accepting passport applications and Selective Service registration forms. DHS officials discussed broadly how DHS is often colocated with USDA, the Drug Enforcement Administration (DEA) and the Federal Bureau of Investigation (FBI) because those agencies have complementary missions to certain DHS operations. These colocations take place in both GSA-held and DHS-held space. While not inter-agency, Interior officials described how the agency has tried to colocate its various bureaus for the sake of agency synergies, especially since the public often does not distinguish among the roles of the bureaus. They noted that integrating services in space or function is a good practice that could occur across agencies. USDA officials also said that the colocation of the Farm Service Agency (FSA) and the Natural Resources Conservation Service (NRCS) provided synergies because they are able to share databases and pass information more readily between the two entities.

Federal officials also said that, under certain circumstances, colocation could result in cost savings or avoidance for the federal government. For example, DHS officials described the department's examination of colocation opportunities within the department, and cited one case it studied where cost savings could result from productivity gains, reduced redundancy, and cost avoidance. USPS officials in multiple locations noted USPS would benefit from revenue from a federal agency tenant. For example, USPS could share underutilized floor and retail window space with other government agencies, generating revenue to offset some building costs. Additionally, GSA officials described the motivation to accomplish savings from consolidation and colocation as responsible asset stewardship.

While federal officials seemed to agree that colocation can produce efficiencies, data limitations, such as the lack of a national, multi-agency asset-management tool as discussed in the next section, make it difficult to estimate the financial and nonfinancial benefits from colocating federal agencies, because the quality of any estimate is a direct function of the input data. Moreover, colocation will not always be more cost-effective than leasing in the short run, particularly if the costs to reconfigure owned space are high. For example, DOD officials said that it cost $20 million to renovate a vacant 70,000-square-foot warehouse within the Naval Support Facility in suburban north Philadelphia and move the Navy Human Resources Service Center there from leased commercial space. They estimated that the payback period for the move would exceed 30 years. Information on cost and service delivery improvements from colocations can help agencies decide whether to proceed with colocations and aid agencies in evaluating completed colocations. Generally, however, agencies lack the tools—such as a standardized approach for quantifying costs and benefits—to determine whether, and to what extent, colocations will generate or are generating intended savings or financial benefits, metrics that are key to helping agencies manage their resources. Moreover, some federal officials indicated that quantitatively measuring the nonfinancial results of colocations, such as intergovernmental collaboration, was difficult to do because these are difficult concepts to monetize, as they can be subjective. We found that agencies generally lacked the tools to measure the costs and benefits of colocation efforts. Our work on capital decision making has shown that establishing an analytical framework for review, approval, and selection of projects; evaluating a project's results; and incorporating lessons learned into the decision-making process are all key principles and practices of such an effort.[26] Establishing a framework with a mixture of financial and nonfinancial benefits, such as service delivery improvements, allows entities to better evaluate performance.

GREATER INTER-AGENCY COLLABORATION COULD MITIGATE SOME CHALLENGES TO COLOCATION

Agency officials said that greater collaboration—through strategic partnerships among federal agencies targeted to meet specific needs and a formal local coordination mechanism—could mitigate some administrative, financial and data challenges to colocation. Agencies' varying real property-management authorities can create administrative challenges, which officials said could be addressed through a strategic partnership with GSA. Acquiring the needed up-front financing for repair or renovation remains challenging for agencies, although some agencies have secured up-front financing through partnerships with private entities. Agencies face challenges identifying colocation opportunities because of limitations with available data and the lack of a coordination mechanism. Officials from a few agencies suggested that structured local or regional coordination could best identify opportunities where the missions of various agencies could be "matched" to appropriate space because of local and regional federal officials' more detailed knowledge of local needs, conditions, and opportunities.

Administrative Challenges

Agencies have varying real property management authorities related to colocation, including the ability to share property and retain the proceeds, and this variation can create administrative challenges for agencies seeking to increase inter-agency colocation opportunities. For example, USPS can share its property with private or government entities and retain the proceeds,[27] but other agencies may not be able to do so.[28] DOE officials reported that the agency is allowed, under certain circumstances, to share government-owned real property, but it is not allowed to retain the proceeds, unless provided for in its annual appropriation. In addition, even if an agency has the authority to share real property, it may not be well-prepared to handle tasks such as setting lease rates and managing the financial arrangements for renovations. For example, GSA officials said some agencies do not know what rates to charge for the space they would share with other agencies. Moreover, Navy officials said agencies with the authority to share properties can face administrative challenges managing the many various sources of funds potentially needed should extensive renovations be necessary to bring properties up to usable condition.

Officials from six agencies as well as commercial real estate officials said that to overcome some of these administrative challenges and improve colocation efforts, agencies could address specific challenges through a strategic partnership with GSA. They said GSA has administrative structures and experiences that could benefit less-experienced agencies. For example, GSA, as the federal government's property manager, already possesses the capability to market and price properties and manage leases on a large scale. Our previous work on the Government Performance and Results Act (GPRA)[29] also supports the idea that strategic partnerships could be beneficial to overcoming these challenges. We have reported that cross-government agency collaboration can produce more public value than can be produced when agencies act alone.[30] Specifically, agencies can enhance and sustain their collaborative efforts by engaging in a variety of practices[31] such as establishing policies and procedures to operate across agency boundaries, by, for example, developing interagency handbooks that define common standards, policies, and procedures. During our review, officials from four agencies suggested that increased collaboration through some of these practices could help mitigate some of the administrative challenges of colocation. As a potential approach for these types of strategic partnerships, OMB officials described GSA's effort to work with selected agencies to develop strategic plans for future property needs and identify potential areas for consolidation.

USPS has some experience collaborating with other agencies on real property issues, and as it explores further options to better utilize excess space, strategic partnerships with other agencies, particularly GSA, could help USPS overcome administrative challenges that may be impeding colocation. A February 2012 USPS OIG report said USPS has experience with intergovernmental collaboration because it already shares space in federal buildings and conducts transactions for other federal entities. 32 For example, the Mansfield, Ohio, federal building hosts a post office as well as offices of SSA, the Internal Revenue Service (IRS), and the U.S. Department of Labor. The report noted that because many postal facilities are near many GSA-leased properties, sharing space could potentially lower overall federal lease costs. The report recognized USPS's need to optimize its network through internal consolidations and closures, but said USPS could use its underutilized resources better through external collaboration. USPS management agreed with the OIG recommendation to develop and implement a strategy to address these findings.

Financial Challenges

During our site visits, we found federally owned properties that could be made available for leasing; however, many of the spaces would need substantial repair or renovation, and acquiring the needed up-front financing remains challenging for agencies.[33] For example, we saw several USPS properties in which the available space required substantial renovation to replace old carpet, peeling paint, and outdated fixtures, and to repair water damage (see fig. 4). However, USPS's deteriorating financial condition may limit the costs it can incur to renovate its facilities prior to sharing them with other agencies.[34]

Upstairs offices in the Easton Main Post Office with walls, ceilings and floors damaged by water.
Source: GAO.

Figure 4. Vacant USPS Space in Easton, Pennsylvania, Requiring Renovation.

We also observed spaces that would need potentially costly specialized repairs or renovations. For example, some of the U.S. Navy properties we visited at the mixed-use Philadelphia Navy Yard (see fig. 5) would need asbestos abatement and water damage repair. Navy officials told us that the properties could be leased from the Navy by other government agencies, and that some agencies have made inquiries to do so. However, they said that the agencies were alarmed by the complexity and costs of repairs, which effectively ended any further consideration of the properties for colocation. Had any agencies pursued leasing the properties, Navy officials said they likely would lack sufficient up-front financing. In addition to general and specialized renovation costs, Navy officials said DOD Unified Facilities Criteria (UFC) requirements prescribe certain antiterrorism measures, such as blast-proof windows and security gates, which can further elevate the costs of renovations to DOD-owned buildings, both on and off-base.

Source: GAO.

Figure 5. Building 1 at the Philadelphia Navy Yard: Exterior, Interior Unfinished, Interior Finished.

The up-front costs of renovations present a challenge to GSA that hinders its colocation efforts. GSA regional officials said that financing renovations is the most serious challenge they face in improving the utilization of their assets. Regional officials said they have considered acquiring vacant USPS facilities that could support colocation, but have been reluctant to do so in part because of the up-front cost of the extensive renovations needed to make the properties usable. As we have previously reported, in recent years budgeting and appropriations decisions, made by the executive branch and Congress, have limited the amount of resources made available from the Federal Buildings Fund to GSA to fund real property operations, acquisition, and maintenance.[35] GSA headquarters officials told us that these limitations make it challenging for the agency to effectively manage its portfolio and result in delayed or cancelled projects.

A private entity took title of and renovated the 1935 building, and now leases it back to the federal government.

Source: GAO.

Figure 6. The Former Downtown Philadelphia USPS Mail Processing and Distribution Center, Now IRS Offices.

In an era of resource constraints and competing priorities, some agencies have secured up-front financing through partnerships with private entities. Federal officials suggested that such strategic partnerships have helped agencies respond to financial challenges associated with renovations, although our previous work has shown this option generally adds expense. Both GSA and USPS cited previous IRS consolidations into underutilized USPS properties in Kansas City and Philadelphia that were arranged using private financing to overcome a lack of up-front federal funding. These arrangements involved multiple stakeholders and were large-scale, complex arrangements designed to replace outdated regional IRS offices (see fig. 6). [36] Private real estate development and GSA regional officials said that if GSA had access to up-front funding to renovate the building, the Philadelphia arrangement would not have been necessary, and the property could have remained in the federal inventory.[37] This outcome would have made redevelopment more cost-efficient for the government in the long-term, because as we have reported, renovations financed by the private sector will generally cost more than those financed by Treasury borrowing.[38]

Data Challenges

The only national-level, multi-agency real property database—the FRPP—was not designed to be an active asset management system.[39]

As such, it does not possess the level of detail necessary to support the identification of colocation opportunities. The FRPP can provide basic descriptive information about the government's federal property holdings, such as address, square footage and facility type; however, colocation decisions would require more data elements than would be practical to add to the FRPP. For example, the FRPP provides square footage information, but it does not provide information on orientation or use of space. We visited a DHS-held site where most of the facility was underground and much of the unoccupied space was used by environmental systems such as air filtration units and pumps that could not be removed. (See fig. 7.) The FRPP does not reveal that the facility is underground, nor does it convey the substantial challenges to reconfiguring the space. Similarly, we found that one building under renovation was characterized as "underutilized" in the FRPP. While not technically incorrect, characterizing this space as underutilized can be misleading because the simple utilization designation does not necessarily indicate if the space can be immediately occupied or used for colocation.

The FRPP does not capture when "underutilized" buildings are under renovation (left) or when spaces cannot be occupied, such as areas used for environmental systems at an underground facility (right).
Source: GAO.

Figure 7. Examples of Federally Held Spaces Described in the FRPP.

As a result, local and regional federal officials are generally better positioned than headquarters officials to manage the colocation process because of their more detailed knowledge of local needs, conditions, and opportunities. We found that detailed property knowledge necessary to facilitate colocations was concentrated at the regional and local levels, rather than at headquarters. When we asked for detailed information about specific properties, we were referred to local and regional federal officials, who were knowledgeable about specific sites and facilities. Some headquarters officials were familiar with attempts at colocation and could describe overall situations, but they were not the primary contacts for these efforts, nor could they readily describe the properties' attributes or local office needs. In general, local and regional federal officials said that they knew property details—such as space configuration, access routes, and parking availability—that would be important for facilitating colocations.[40] In addition, FRPC, which created the FRPP database, is a national, policy-oriented body. As such, the scope of FRPC's mission does not include managing the local-level negotiations that colocation would require.

The detailed property knowledge held by local federal officials is important for ensuring an appropriate match between the agency that owns the property and the agency that would lease space. Officials from many agencies reported that matching the location of available property to the mission and security needs of the agency searching for space is an important consideration; for example, DOE's need for isolated, remote sites as compared to VA's

interest in sites readily accessible to veterans. However, officials noted that
that there are no universal requirements regarding their respective agencies'
property needs—rather, the property needs vary across the country in response
to mission needs. In some cases, agencies have operational requirements that
would make colocation inappropriate if the potential tenant and potential
lessor did not share the same mission needs. For example, USPS officials
noted the Postal Service's need to keep mail secure and separate from potential
tenant agencies or members of the public who may need to access the facility.
Additionally, officials from DOD told us that in some circumstances their
security requirements would make them ill-suited to share space with other
agencies, such as when public access would be required. However, in
instances where mission needs were similar, potential tenants might see
enhanced security as desirable.

In other cases, an agency's mission may dictate the need for a specialized
facility that could make colocation inappropriate. For example, USDA
officials in a few regions told us that farmers often drove farm vehicles,
including tractors, to Service Center locations and that in these cases,
underground parking in a federal building would be problematic. In addition,
we visited a leased Interior site that required a blacksmith and carpentry shop,
cold storage for artifacts, and parking for large maintenance vehicles, such as
wood-chippers and industrial mowers (see photos in fig. 8 below). An Interior
official said that these needs would have to be taken into account to share
space. None of these details are included in the FRPP, but local and regional
officials from several agencies noted that they can speak readily on how
mission needs and facility details may impact colocation.

Interior carpentry space to repair historic design elements of Park Service property
    (left), a cold storage locker (center), and one of Interior's maintenance vehicles
    stored on-site (right).
Source: GAO.

Figure 8. Examples of Spaces Used by Interior at a Leased Site.

Officials from several agencies acknowledged that property knowledge is sometimes communicated informally. However, various officials noted that the lack of a systematic mechanism to share information hinders any efforts to colocate. Officials from a few agencies suggested that structured local or regional coordination could best identify opportunities where the missions of various agencies could be "matched" to appropriate space. Several local officials who showed us vacant federal spaces said there is currently no online or formal mechanism they can use to share vacancy details with officials from other agencies who might need space. A previous effort at local coordination—the Governmentwide Real Property Information Sharing program (GRPIS)—experienced some success, according to GSA officials, which they attributed to connections made at the local level. The program was tasked with encouraging and facilitating the sharing of real property information among federal agencies, and it revolved around the formation of real property councils within major federal communities nationwide. GSA officials said that local councils were an effective method for sharing information. However, officials said the program became essentially inactive after responsibility for the program was transferred within GSA and local connections were lost.

CONCLUSION

Colocating federal agencies into government-owned space represents an opportunity to improve government operations while simultaneously addressing two of the federal government's long-standing real-property management challenges: reducing over-reliance on costly leasing and the presence of underutilized owned property. Our analysis of eight markets shows that there are underutilized owned properties near areas where the government also leases space for other purposes. However, colocations are far more complicated than just matching the square feet needed with the square feet available. Agencies' mission needs and building-specific issues that include security, condition, configuration, and use must align for the colocation to fully succeed. FRPC has coordinated federal real property actions for almost a decade at the national level, but detailed local knowledge of agency missions and facility needs combined with systematic communication channels are needed to match owners with compatible tenants.

Once matched, numerous capacity and administrative hurdles remain as challenges to successful colocation. GSA is the only agency that has a core mission of managing real property. Several landholding agencies lack the experience and administrative tools necessary to effectively market and manage their property as a landlord. Creating cross-agency relationships with GSA to assist in tasks such as setting rental rates, crafting lease documents, renovating space, and otherwise managing the property would improve consistency of approach and allow each agency to remain focused on its core mission.

Colocation is not always the right answer. We found that agencies can force relocations into ill-suited locations, pushing the financial breakeven point out decades into the future. Without the tools to measure the benefits and costs of colocation efforts or proposals, policy makers are unable to effectively weigh colocation as an option. Understanding the financial costs and savings associated with colocation efforts, as well as the nature and extent of synergies and improved services, will allow agencies to better demonstrate that the benefits can be worth the costs of renovating and moving an agency out of privately leased space.

RECOMMENDATIONS FOR EXECUTIVE ACTION

To promote colocation across agencies, the Director of the Office of Management and Budget (OMB) should work with the Federal Real Property Council (FRPC) and the U.S. Postal Service (USPS) to implement GAO's three recommendations:

- Establish a mechanism, which includes USPS, for local coordination in markets with large concentrations of federal agencies to identify, on a case by case basis, specific opportunities to share space and improve coordination of real property use across agencies.
- Develop strategic partnerships and a coordinated strategy with assigned roles and tasks between the General Services Administration (GSA) and other federal landholding agencies (USPS specifically) with less experience sharing real property.
- Develop and implement tools, along with supporting guidance, to measure, evaluate, and disseminate information on financial and nonfinancial benefits, such as service delivery improvements, from colocating federal agencies.

AGENCY COMMENTS

We provided a draft of this report to OMB, GSA, USPS, VA, USDA, DOE, Interior, DHS, DOD, and IRS for review and comment. In commenting on a draft of this report, officials from OMB said that they agreed with the report's findings, conclusions, and recommendations and offered technical comments that we incorporated as appropriate. They said that OMB has little power over how USPS manages its real property assets. The officials also said that GSA has already started looking at consolidating tenant field operations within its portfolio, and suggested that the report clarify the role that we recommend GSA takes in facilitating consolidations. USPS agreed with the facts and findings in the report and provided comments regarding our recommendations. GSA agreed with our recommendations and provided technical comments that we incorporated as appropriate. DHS and VA provided clarifying technical comments which we incorporated, where appropriate. USDA, DOE, Interior, DHS, DOD, and IRS did not provide comments.

Sincerely yours,

David J. Wise
Director, Physical Infrastructure Issues

APPENDIX I: SCOPE AND METHODOLOGY

Our objective was to review the issues surrounding colocation—that is, moving federal operations from one stand-alone location to a federal location occupied by another entity.[1] To accomplish this, we addressed (1) if the potential for cross-agency colocation exists, what factors can affect that potential; (2) the potential benefits of colocation; and (3) the challenges associated with colocation, and what solutions, if any, can mitigate these challenges. During the course of our work we used the Federal Real Property Portfolio (FRPP), a government-wide database of owned and leased space, maintained by GSA on behalf of the Federal Real Property Council (FRPC). We recently reported that the FRPC has not followed sound data collection practices—related to data consistency, performance measures, collaboration, and data reporting—when collecting FRPP data, that would help them collect these data in a way that is sufficiently consistent and accurate to be useful making property management decisions.[2] We recommended that GSA develop a plan to improve the FRPP consistent with sound data collection practices. Nonetheless, we also reported that the FRPP can be used in a general sense to track assets. As such, for this report, we used FRPP data for the limited purposes of identifying agencies within our scope, selecting case study markets and summarizing agency-level statistics on owned and leased property.

We used the 2010 Federal Real Property Portfolio (FRPP) summary report and U.S. Postal Service property data to identify the agencies which hold the largest amounts of property. We then limited our scope to 8 of the top 10 agencies, which include the Departments of Agriculture (USDA), Defense (DOD), Energy (DOE), Homeland Security (DHS), the Interior (Interior), Veterans Affairs (VA), the General Services Administration (GSA), and the U.S. Postal Service (USPS).[3]

To determine the factors that can affect cross-agency consolidation, we analyzed detailed data and interviewed agency officials about the property holdings in 8 specific U.S. markets: Allentown PA, Cleveland OH, Dallas TX, Kansas City KS, Kerrville TX, Philadelphia PA, San Antonio TX, and Waco TX. To select these areas and provide nationwide statistics on owned and leased facilities, we analyzed basic inventory data, including location, occupant, size, owned/leased data from the FRPP for the 7 agencies in our scope that are represented in the FRPP. USPS, which is not represented in the FRPP, provided data from its internal systems. While case studies are not generalizable, we selected diverse markets in terms of market size, geographic region, owned and leased federal properties, and agencies present. Although we used GSA-defined markets as a guideline, to better reflect the interests of this review we delineated markets by using an estimated 60-minute commute radius, and selected the borders based on professional judgment (for example, in more rural areas, following the direction of development.) We identified the primary cities of large and medium markets using GSA data, and then selected small markets within driving distance of a large or medium-sized market in order to facilitate travel.

Because there are no reliable real property cost and benefit data, we primarily relied on interviews with federal agency officials at the national, regional, and local levels to determine the potential benefits of colocation. We focused on benefits that were mentioned by officials from more than one agency and more than one market. We also reviewed relevant GAO and other reports and documents, including USPS Office of Inspector General reports, and laws, regulations, and guidance.

To determine the challenges associated with colocation and what solutions, if any, could mitigate these challenges, we visited facilities that were both owned and leased, with a particular emphasis on owned offices and warehouses that were categorized as underutilized.[4] We did not include properties categorized as inactive, excess, or disposed in our scope, and we did not include land. Using this information, we conducted an analysis to identify key challenges that agencies face when making property decisions and the options, if any, for mitigating those challenges.

We also interviewed agency officials at the national, regional, and local level, and reviewed documentation provided to us regarding specific properties. We did not examine any screenings for other potential uses of real property, such as use for the homeless or public benefit. To determine which challenges were the most pressing, we only included challenges which were raised in more than one market and by more than one agency.

We conducted this performance audit from July 2011 through July 2012 in accordance with generally accepted government auditing standards. Those standards require that we plan and perform the audit to obtain sufficient, appropriate evidence to provide a reasonable basis for our findings and conclusions based on our audit objectives. We believe that the evidence obtained provides a reasonable basis for our findings and conclusions based on our audit objectives.

APPENDIX II: SELECTED LEASING AND RETENTION OF PROCEEDS AUTHORITIES FOR IN-SCOPE AGENCIES

This list is not intended to be inclusive of all of an agency's real property authorities; there may be other authorities not included below that may authorize colocation.

Agency	Relevant statute and description of authority
Agriculture (USDA)	*Enhanced Use Lease Authority Pilot Program* *7 U.S.C. § 3125a note* The Secretary of Agriculture is authorized to establish a pilot program and lease nonexcess real property at the Beltsville Agricultural Research Center and the National Agricultural Library to any individual or entity, including agencies or

Agency	Relevant statute and description of authority
	instrumentalities of State or local governments, if the Secretary determines that the lease is consistent with, and will not adversely affect, the mission of the agency administering the property; will enhance the use of the property; will not permit any portion of the property or facility to be used for the public retail or wholesale sale of merchandise or residential development; will not permit the construction or modification of facilities financed by nonfederal sources to be used by an agency, except for incidental use; and will not include any property or facility required for any agency purpose without prior consideration of the needs of the agency. Consideration for any lease shall be for fair market value and for cash. The Secretary is authorized to enter into leases until June 18, 2013, and the term of the lease shall not exceed 30 years.[a] *Retention of Proceeds/Enhanced Use Lease Authority Pilot Program* *7 U.S.C. § 3125a note* Consideration for leases shall be deposited in a capital asset account, which is available until expended, without further appropriation, for maintenance, capital revitalization, and improvements to the department's properties and facilities at the Beltsville Agricultural Research Center and the National Agricultural Library.
Defense (DOD)[b]	*Leases of Non-Excess Property of Military Departments* *10 U.S.C. § 2667* The Secretary of a military department is authorized to lease nonexcess real property under the control of the department that is not needed for public use if the Secretary considers the lease to be advantageous to the United States and upon such terms that will promote the national defense or be in the public interest. The term of the lease may not be more than 5 years, unless the Secretary determines the term should be longer to promote the national defense or to be in the public interest. Lease payments shall be in cash or in-kind consideration for an amount not less than fair market value. In-kind consideration includes maintenance, protection, alteration, repair, or environmental restoration of property or facilities; construction of new facilities; providing facilities;

Appendix II. (Continued)

Agency	Relevant statute and description of authority
	or providing or paying for utility services.

Retention of Proceeds/Leases of Non-Excess Property of Military Departments
10 U.S.C. § 2667
Proceeds from leases of a military department are deposited into a special account in the Treasury and are available to the Secretary of that military department for such activities as maintenance, protection, alteration, or environmental restoration of property or facilities; construction of new facilities; lease of facilities; or payment of utility services. At least 50 percent of the proceeds received shall be available for activities at the military installations where the proceeds are derived. Prior to fiscal year 2005, any amounts deposited in a special account from the disposition of property were only available as provided in an appropriation act. Beginning in fiscal year 2005, any amounts deposited into a special account from the disposition of property are appropriated and available for obligation or available to the Secretary without additional congressional action.[c]

Conveyance or Lease of Existing Property and Facilities
10 U.S.C. § 2878
The Secretary concerned is authorized to convey or lease property or facilities, including ancillary supporting facilities to eligible entities at such consideration the Secretary concerned considers appropriate for the purposes of the alternative authority for acquisition and improvement of military housing and to protect the interests of the United States.[d]

Retention of Proceeds/Conveyance or Lease of Existing Property and Facilities
10 U.S.C. § 2883
Proceeds from the conveyance or lease of property or facilities under 10 U.S.C. § 2878 shall be credited to the Department of Defense Housing Improvement Funds.

Agency	Relevant statute and description of authority
	Proceeds may be used to carry out activities with respect to the alternative authority for the acquisition and improvement of military housing, including activities required in connection with the planning, execution, and administration of contracts subject to such amounts as provided in appropriation acts.
Energy (DOE)	*Leasing of Property* *42 U.S.C. § 7256* The Secretary of Energy is authorized to lease acquired real property located at a DOE facility that is to be closed or reconfigured and is not needed by DOE at the time the lease is entered into if the Secretary considers the lease to be appropriate to promote national security or is in the public interest. The term of the lease may be up to 10 years, with an option to renew the lease for another 10 years, if the Secretary determines that a renewal of the lease will promote national security or be in the public interest. Lease payments may be in cash or in-kind consideration and may be for an amount less than fair market value. In kind consideration may include services relating to the protection and maintenance of the leased property. *Retention of Proceeds/Leasing of Property* *42 U.S.C. § 7256* To the extent provided in advance in appropriations acts, the Secretary is authorized to use the funds received as rents to cover administrative expenses of the lease, maintenance and repair of the leased property, or environmental restoration activities at the facility where the leased property is located.
General Services Administration (GSA)	*Disposition of Real Property* *40 U.S.C. § 543* The Administrator of GSA is authorized to dispose of surplus real property by sale, exchange, lease, permit, or transfer for cash, credit, or other property. *Conveyance of Property Consolidated Appropriations Act of 2005, Pub. L. No. 108-447, §412, 118 Stat. 2809, 3259 (2004)*

Appendix II. (Continued)

Agency	Relevant statute and description of authority
	The Administrator of GSA, notwithstanding any other provision of law, is authorized to convey by sale, lease, exchange, or otherwise, including through leaseback arrangements, real and related personal property, or interests therein.
	Retention of Proceeds/Conveyance of Property Consolidated Appropriations Act of 2005, Pub. L. No. 108-447, § 412, 118 Stat. 2809, 3259 (2004) Net proceeds from the disposition of real property are deposited in GSA's Federal Buildings Fund (FBF) and are used for GSA real property capital needs to the extent provided in appropriations acts.
Homeland Security (DHS/U.S. Coast Guard)	*General Powers of the Commandant, U.S. Coast Guard 14 U.S.C. § 93(a)(13)* The U.S. Coast Guard may rent or lease real property, not required for immediate use, for a period not exceeding 5 years. Payments received from the rental or lease, less amount of expenses incurred (exclusive of governmental personal services), to be deposited in the Treasury.
Interior (DOI)	*Leases for National Park System (NPS) 16 U.S.C. § 1a-2(k)(1)-(4)* Interior is authorized to enter into a lease with any person or governmental entity for the use of buildings and associated property administered by the Secretary as part of the National Park System. Leases shall be for fair market value rental. Buildings and associated property leased shall be used for an activity that is consistent with the purposes established by law for the unit in which the building is located; shall not result in degradation of the purposes and values of the unit; and shall be compatible with National Park Service programs. *Retention of Proceeds/Leases for NPS 16 U.S.C. § 1a-2(k)(5)*

Agency	Relevant statute and description of authority
	Rental payments must be deposited into a special Treasury account where the availability of funds is not subject to an appropriation act. Funds are available for infrastructure needs such as facility refurbishment, repair and replacement, infrastructure projects associated with park resource protection, and direct maintenance of the leased buildings and associated properties. *Leases for Housing NPS employees* *16 U.S.C. § 17o* Interior is authorized where necessary and justified to make available employee housing, on or off the lands under the administrative jurisdiction of the National Park Service, and to rent or lease such housing to field employees of the National Park Service at rates based on the reasonable value of the housing. *Housing for NPS employees* *16 U.S.C. § 17o* Subject to the appropriation of necessary funds in advance, Interior is authorized to lease federal lands and interests in land to qualified persons for up to 50 years for the construction of field employee quarters. *Presidio of San Francisco* *16 U.S.C. § 460bb note* The Presidio Trust is authorized to enter into leases with any person, firm, association, organization, corporation or governmental entity necessary to carry out its authorized activities. The Presidio Trust is authorized to establish procedures for lease agreements for the use and occupancy of Presidio facilities. The National Park Service or any other Federal agency is authorized to enter into leases with the Presidio Trust which are necessary and appropriate.
Postal Service (USPS)	*USPS Real Property Authorities* *39 U.S.C. § 401(5)* The Postal Service is authorized to acquire in any legal manner, real property or any interest therein, as it deems necessary or convenient in the transaction of its business and

Appendix II. (Continued)

Agency	Relevant statute and description of authority
	to hold, maintain, sell, lease, or otherwise dispose of such property or any interest therein. *USPS Real Property Authorities* *39 U.S.C. § 401(6)* The Postal Service is authorized to construct, operate, lease, and maintain buildings, facilities, or equipment, and to make other improvements on any property owned or controlled by it. *USPS Retention of Proceeds/Real Property Authorities* *39 U.S.C. §§ 2003, 2401* Proceeds are deposited into the Postal Service Fund and remain available to the Postal Service without fiscal year limitation to carry out the purposes, functions, and powers of the Postal Service. All revenues received by the Postal Service are appropriated to the Postal Service and are available without additional congressional action.
Veterans Affairs (VA)	*VA Transfer Authority – Capital Asset Fund* *38 U.S.C. § 8118* The Secretary of VA is authorized to transfer real property under VA's control or custody to another department or agency of the United States, to a state or political subdivision of a state, or to any public or private entity, including an Indian tribe until December 31, 2018. The property must be transferred for fair market value, unless it is transferred to a homeless provider. Property under this authority cannot be disposed of until the Secretary determines that the property is no longer needed by the department in carrying out its functions and is not suitable for use for the provision of services to homeless veterans by the department under the McKinney-Vento Act. *Authority to Outlease* *38 U.S.C. § 8122* The Secretary may lease for a term not exceeding 3 years

Agency	Relevant statute and description of authority
	lands or buildings, or parts or parcels thereof, belonging to the United States and under the Secretary's control. A lease made to any public or nonprofit organization may provide for the maintenance, protection, or restoration, by the lessee, of the property leased, as a part or all of the consideration for the lease. Prior to the execution of any such lease, the Secretary shall give appropriate public notice of the Secretary's intention to do so in the newspaper of the community in which the lands or buildings to be leased are located. The proceeds from such leases (less expenses for maintenance, operation, and repair of buildings leased for living quarters) shall be turned over to the Treasury of the United States as miscellaneous receipts. *Retention of Proceeds/Transfer Authority* *38 U.S.C. § 8118* Proceeds from the transfer of real property are deposited into the VA Capital Asset Fund and, to the extent provided in advance in appropriations acts, may be used for property transfer costs such as demolition, environmental remediation, and maintenance and repair; costs associated with future transfers of property under this authority; costs associated with enhancing medical care services to veterans by improving, renovating, replacing, updating, or establishing patient care facilities through minor construction projects; and costs associated with the transfer or adaptive use of property that is under the Secretary's jurisdiction and listed on the National Register of Historic Places.

Source: GAO analysis

[a] This pilot program was enacted in the Food, Conservation, and Energy Act of 2008, Pub. L. No. 110- 246, § 7409, 112 Stat. 1651, 2014-2016 (2008).

[b] Our review of DOD did not include real property at a military installation designated for closure or realignment under a base closure law. Therefore, for purposes of this appendix we have excluded DOD authorities relating to base closure or realignment. Additionally, while some authorities in this enclosure, such as 10 U.S.C. § 2667, contain subsections relating to base closure and realignment, for purposes of this enclosure we are referring to the other subsections of the statute.

[c] Department of Defense Appropriations Act for Fiscal Year 2005, Pub. L. No. 108-287, § 8034, 118 Stat. 951, 978 (2004).

[d] This authority does not apply to property or facilities located on or near a military installation approved for closure under a base closure law. See 10 U.S.C. § 2878(b).

End Notes

[1] According to the Federal Real Property Council's most recent Federal Real Property Report, which provided summary-level reports on governmentwide real property data, as of September 30, 2010. This data is reported at the asset level, not the lease level, meaning that while portions of a building are leased, the entire building is counted as an asset.

[2] GAO, *Federal Real Property: Proposed Civilian Board Could Address Disposal of Unneeded Facilities*, GAO-11-704T (Washington, D.C.: June 9, 2011).

[3] GAO's high-risk series identifies areas at high risk due to their greater vulnerabilities to waste, fraud, abuse, and mismanagement or major challenges associated with their economy, efficiency, or effectiveness. See GAO, *High-Risk Series: An Update*, GAO-11-278 (Washington, D.C.: Feb. 16, 2011).

[4] E.g., Civilian Property Realignment Act of 2012, S. 2232, 112th Cong. (2012); Civilian Property Realignment Act, H.R. 1734, 112th Cong. (2011).

[5] Federal Real Property Asset Management Reform Act of 2012, S. 2178, 112th Cong. (2012).

[6] 21st Century Postal Service Act of 2012, S. 1789, 112th Cong. (2012).

[7] Office of Management and Budget, *Promoting Efficient Spending to Support Agency Operations (M-12-12).* (May 11, 2012).

[8] We recently reported that the FRPC has not followed sound data collection practices— related to data consistency, performance measures, collaboration, and data reporting— when collecting FRPP data, that would help it collect these data in a way that is sufficiently consistent and accurate to be useful making property management decisions. See GAO, *Federal Real Property: Improved Data and a National Strategy Needed to Address the Excess and Underutilized Property Problem,* GAO-12-645 (Washington, D.C.: June 20, 2012). We recommended that GSA develop a plan to improve the FRPP consistent with sound data collection practices. Nonetheless, we also reported that the FRPP is sufficiently reliable to be used in a general sense to track assets. As such, for this report, we used FRPP data for the limited purposes of identifying case study markets and summarizing agency-level statistics on owned and leased property.

[9] Only the 24 federal agencies subject to the Chief Financial Officers (CFO) Act of 1990 are required to submit real property data at the constructed asset level to the FRPP on an annual basis under Executive Order 13327. GSA is counted as one of the 24 agencies. The Departments of Education, Housing and Urban Development; the Small Business Administration; the Nuclear Regulatory Commission; and the Social Security Administration obtain and use real estate through GSA. Consequently, GSA reports those real property assets. DOD is also counted as a reporting agency and reports property data for the Army, Air Force, Navy, and Corps of Engineers. USPS is not required to submit real property data to the FRPP and is therefore not included in this data. See, Federal Real Property Council, *FY 2010 Federal Real Property Report: An Overview of the U.S. Federal Government's Real Property Assets.*

[10] Otherwise-managed buildings may be owned by a state government or by a foreign government that has granted rights for use to the federal government in an arrangement other than a lease agreement.

[11] USDA, DOE, GSA-"leased," Interior, VA data are from fiscal year 2010, DHS and GSA-"owned" data are from fiscal year 2011, and USPS data are from fiscal year 2012.

[12] See, for example, GAO, *General Services Administration: Comparison of Space Acquisition Alternatives—Leasing to Lease-Purchase and Leasing to Construction*, GAO/GGD-99-49R (Washington, D.C.: Mar. 12, 1999) and *General Services Administration: Opportunities For Cost Savings in the Public Buildings Area*, GAO/T-GGD-95-149 (Washington, D.C.: July 13, 1995).

[13] See GAO, *Federal Real Property: Overreliance on Leasing Contributed to High-Risk Designation*, GAO-11-879T (Washington, D.C.: Aug. 4, 2011). GSA income statement losses within the leased inventory, as measured by funds from operations (FFO), increased dramatically in recent years to $102.9 million in fiscal year 2009 before falling to $64.8 million in fiscal year 2010. FFO is derived by calculating the amount of revenue remaining after deducting all direct and indirect expenses (excluding depreciation) associated with operating a building, and provides the Federal Buildings Fund with contributions to capital towards future investments in renovations, repairs, and new construction.

[14] According to GSA, losses in leased inventory are partially attributable to the accounting treatment of different rent payments and fees in accordance with financial statement reporting requirements, but the agency should still be able to cover all the extra costs with the administrative fee it charges tenant agencies.

[15] 40 U.S.C. § 585.

[16] Federal Real Property Asset Management, Exec. Order No. 13327, 69 Fed. Reg. 5897 (Feb. 6, 2004).

[17] The executive order applies to the Departments of Agriculture (USDA), Commerce, Defense, Education, Energy, Health and Human Services, Homeland Security, Housing and Urban Development, Interior, Justice, Labor, State, Transportation, the Treasury, Veterans Affairs (VA); the Environmental Protection Agency; the National Aeronautics and Space Administration; the United States Agency for International Development; the General Services Administration (GSA); the National Science Foundation, the Nuclear Regulatory Commission; the Office of Personnel Management; the Small Business Administration; and the Social Security Administration.

[18] See, for example, GAO, *Federal Real Property: Progress Made Toward Addressing Problems, but Underlying Obstacles Continue to Hamper Reform*, GAO-07-349 (Washington, D.C.: Apr. 13, 2007*); Federal Real Property: Proposed Civilian Board Could Address Disposal of Unneeded Facilities*, GAO11-704T (Washington, D.C.: June 9, 2011) and *High-Risk Series: An Update*, GAO-11-278 (Washington, D.C.: February 2011).

[19] Section 102 of Title 40 of the United States Code defines excess property as "property under the control of a federal agency that the head of the agency determines is not required to meet the agency's needs or responsibilities." GSA's federal management regulations defines underutilized property as "an entire property or portion thereof, with or without improvements, which is used—(a) Irregularly or intermittently by the accountable Executive agency for current program purposes of that agency; or (b) For current program purposes that can be satisfied with only a portion of the property." 41 C.F.R. § 102-75.50.

[20] 39 U.S.C. §§ 401, 410.

[21] GAO, *U.S. Postal Service: Challenges Related to Restructuring the Postal Service's Retail Network,*GAO-12-433 (Washington, D.C.: Apr. 17, 2012).

[22] USPS is authorized to borrow $3 billion annually and a maximum of $15 billion. 39 U.S.C. § 2005(a). USPS borrows money from the U.S. Treasury via the Federal Financing Bank.

[23] Originally due at the end of fiscal year 2011, USPS's $5.5-billion retiree health benefit payment was delayed until August 1, 2012. Pub. L. No. 112-74 (Dec. 23, 2011).

[24] According to the Postal Reorganization Act of 1970, "[p]ostal rates and fees shall provide sufficient revenue so that the total estimated income and appropriations to the Postal Service will equal as nearly as practicable total estimated costs of the Postal Service." Pub. L. No. 91-375, 84 Stat. 760 (Aug. 12, 1970) (formerly 39 U.S.C. § 3621). See also, *Payments on Unfunded Liability by the U.S. Postal Service to Civil Service Retirement Fund: Hearing Before the Committee on Post Office and Civil Service, United States Senate, on H.R. 29*, 93rd Cong. 73-74 (statement by Post Office and Civil Service Committee Chairman Gale McGee).

[25] United States Postal Service, Office of Inspector General. *21st Century Post Office: Opportunities to Share Excess Resources – Management Advisory*, DA-MA-12-003 (Arlington, VA: Feb. 9, 2012.)

[26] GAO, *Executive Guide: Leading Practices in Capital Decision-Making*, GAO/AIMD-99-32 (Washington, D.C.: Dec. 1998).

[27] USPS is authorized to hold, maintain, sell, lease, or otherwise dispose of such property or any interest therein. 39 U.S.C. § 401(5). USPS is authorized to retain and use all revenues that it receives. 39 U.S.C. § 2401(a).

[28] Appendix II provides more information on selected sharing and retention of proceeds authorities granted to the agencies we included in our review.

[29] Both Congress and the executive branch have recognized the need for improved collaboration across the federal government. Accordingly, in January 2011 the almost twodecades-old Government Performance and Results Act of 1993 (GPRA) was updated with the GPRA Modernization Act of 2010 (GPRAMA). Pub. L. No. 111-352, 124 Stat. 3866 (2011). GPRAMA amends the Government Performance and Results Act of 1993, Pub. L. No. 103-62, 107 Stat. 285 (1993).

[30] See GAO, *Results-Oriented Government: Practices That Can Help Enhance and Sustain Collaboration among Federal Agencies*, GAO-06-15 (Washington, D.C.: Oct. 21, 2005).

[31] Such practices include (1) define and articulate a common outcome; (2) establish mutually reinforcing or joint strategies; (3) identify and address needs by leveraging resources; (4) agree on roles and responsibilities; (5) establish compatible policies, procedures, and other means to operate across agency boundaries; (6) develop mechanisms to monitor, evaluate, and report on results; (7) reinforce agency accountability for collaborative efforts through agency plans and reports; and (8) reinforce individual accountability for collaborative efforts through performance management systems. See GAO-06-15.

[32] United States Postal Service, Office of Inspector General. *21st Century Post Office: Opportunities to Share Excess Resources – Management Advisory*, DA-MA-12-003 (Arlington, VA: February 9, 2012.)

[33] For capital projects, including substantial repairs and renovations, agencies must record budget authority for the full cost of an asset up front. Such up-front funding provides recognition for commitments that are embodied in budgetary decisions and maintains governmentwide fiscal control. However, providing budget authority for the large up-front costs of capital assets creates challenges in an era of resource constraints. See, GAO, *Budget Issues: Alternative Approaches to Finance Federal Capital*, GAO-03-1011 (Washington, D.C.: Aug. 21, 2003).

[34] *See*, for example, GAO-12-433, GAO-11-759T, and GAO-11-278.

[35] GAO, *Federal Buildings Fund: Improved Transparency and Long-term Plan Needed to Clarify Capital Funding Priorities*, GAO-12-646 (Washington, D.C.: Jul. 12, 2012).

[36] In downtown Philadelphia, GSA had considered purchasing USPS' large, underutilized 30th St. Mail Processing and Distribution Center Station, but was dissuaded by the substantial cost of the renovation that would be needed for the building, which was constructed in 1935. Instead, in April 2007, USPS signed a deal with a private developer to renovate nearby facilities and, in August 2007, signed a memorandum of understanding with GSA for private redevelopment of the building into IRS offices. In September 2008, USPS moved its retail operations and distribution unit out of 30th St. into its new facilities. When the 30th St. renovation was complete, IRS moved into the property (see fig. 6). In exchange for financing the $184-million renovation, the developer received all interest and rights from USPS for the 30th St. land, building, and a nearby 1,661-space parking garage, and until August 25, 2030, will receive lease payments from GSA, who in turn will receive rent from IRS.

[37] The decision to lease rather than own space for federal operations is often influenced by factors other than cost-effectiveness, including budget issues. Federal budget-scoring rules require that budget authority for ownership options be recorded fully up front in the budget to appropriately reflect the government's commitment. For GSA operating leases, however, only the budget authority needed to cover the annual lease payments is required. This reduces the up-front funding commitment but generally costs the federal government more over time. See GAO-11-879T.

[38] See GAO-03-1011.

[39] The FRPP was designed to describe the nature, use, and extent of federal real property held by executive branch agencies, except when otherwise required for reasons of national security. Federal Real Property Asset Management, Exec. Order No. 13327, 69 Fed. Reg. 5897 (February 6, 2004).

[40] Although some agencies possess databases with detailed property information, we found that local and regional federal officials still used their personal knowledge. For example, one GSA property manager told us that several specific rooms were better for storage than tenants because janitors used the access hallway to bring the entire building's trash to the dumpsters.

End Notes for Appendix I

[1] For the purposes of this review, we focused on one aspect of colocation, defined as moving government operations from privately-owned leased spaces to spaces owned by the federal government. Although colocation can also be used to describe agencies sharing space leased from the private sector, that interpretation is not used for this report

[2] GAO, *Federal Real Property: Improved Data and a National Strategy Needed to Address the Excess and Underutilized Property Problem,* GAO-12-645 (Washington, D.C.: June 20, 2012).

[3] We did not include the Department of Justice (DOJ) or the Department of State (State) in our scope because some of their holdings were notably inappropriate for colocation, including State's international holdings and DOJ's prisons.

[4] During site visits we excluded DOD properties that agency officials identified as being on secure military installations, as these properties are subject to the Base Realignment and Closure Act (BRAC), and have greater security requirements than average federal buildings.

In: Federal Real Property Management ISBN: 978-1-63321-219-0
Editor: Aaron F. Darby © 2014 Nova Science Publishers, Inc.

Chapter 3

FEDERAL REAL PROPERTY: IMPROVED COST REPORTING WOULD HELP DECISION MAKERS WEIGH THE BENEFITS OF ENHANCED USE LEASING[*]

United States Government Accountability Office

WHY GAO DID THIS STUDY

The federal government owns underutilized properties that are costly to operate, yet challenges exist to closing and disposing of them. To obtain value from these properties, some agencies have used EULs, which are generally long-term agreements to lease property from the federal government in exchange for cash or non-cash consideration. However, agencies also incur costs for EUL programs. We have previously reported that agencies should include all costs associated with programs' activities when assessing their values. This report addresses (1) the extent to which agencies attribute the full benefits and costs of their EULs in their assessments of their EUL programs and (2) the experiences of agencies in using their EUL authority.

GAO reviewed property data and documents from the largest civilian federal real property agencies including four agencies that use EULs—VA,

---

[*] This is an edited, reformatted and augmented version of a United States Government Accountability Office publication, No. GAO-13-14, dated December 2012.

NASA, the Department of State, and the Department of Agriculture—and applicable laws, and regulations and guidance. GAO visited nine sites where agencies were using EULs.

WHAT GAO RECOMMENDS

To promote transparency about EULs, improve decision-making regarding EULs and ensure more accurate accounting of EUL benefits, GAO recommends that OMB coordinate with affected agencies to ensure that agencies consistently attribute all relevant costs associated with EULs to their EUL programs. Agencies generally agreed with our findings and recommendation.

WHAT GAO FOUND

Agency officials told us that enhanced use leases (EUL) help them utilize their underutilized property better; commonly cited benefits include enhanced mission activities, cash rent revenue, and value received through in-kind consideration. However, some agencies we reviewed do not include all costs associated with their EULs when they assess the performance of their EUL programs. Guidance from the Office of Management and Budget (OMB) does not specify what costs agencies should include in their EUL evaluations, resulting in variance among agencies. For example, the Department of Veterans Affairs (VA) and the Department of State do not consistently attribute EUL-related costs of consultant staff who administer the leases, and VA does not attribute various administrative costs that offset EUL benefits. Without fully accounting for all EUL costs, agencies may overstate the net benefits of their EUL programs.

Based on recent agency experiences, EULs may be a viable option for redeveloping underutilized federal real property when disposal is not possible or desirable, but two agencies raised issues pertaining to EUL use that affect their use or budgetary treatment. First, National Aeronautics and Space Administration (NASA) officials said that the limit on its authority to receive in-kind consideration as part of its EUL program has limited its ability to encourage the use of EULs for underutilized NASA property. Specifically, NASA officials said prospective lessees are reluctant to make costly capital improvements to a property that will have to be returned to the government at the end of the lease without other compensation, such as a reduction in cash rent. Second, VA and CBO disagree on the extent to which VA should account for the budget impacts for EULs that could include long-term government commitments. VA has made multi-year commitments with certain EULs without fully reporting them in its budget. Assessing and recognizing the budget impacts of EULs is complicated and may be interpreted differently by agencies with EUL authority. In particular, VA EULs can include long-term commitments that are recognized in the federal budget in different ways.

Source: Swinerton Builders (left) and GAO (right).

Federal Real Property leased through an EUL agreement between VA and Clark Country, Washington to construct a Crisis Triage Center in Vancouver, Washington. Left photo: the vacant site in July 2004. Right photo: the developed site in May 2012.

ABBREVIATIONS

CBO	Congressional Budget Office
Energy	Department of Energy
EUL	enhanced use lease
FRPP	Federal Real Property Profile
GSA	General Services Administration
Interior	Department of Interior
Justice	Department of Justice
NASA	National Aeronautics and Space Administration
OMB	Office of Management and Budget
SLSDC	St. Lawrence Seaway Development Corporation
State	Department of State
TVA	Tennessee Valley Authority

USDA   Department of Agriculture
USPS   United States Postal Service
VA   Department of Veterans Affairs

December 19, 2012

The Honorable Thomas R. Carper
Chairman
Subcommittee on Federal Financial Management, Government
Information, Federal Services, and International Security
Committee on Homeland Security and Governmental Affairs
United States Senate

Dear Mr. Chairman:

The federal government owns many underutilized properties that are costly to operate. However, closing or disposing of them can present challenges, including covering the costs associated with federal real property disposal, addressing legal requirements agencies must adhere to, such as requirements for screening and environmental cleanup, and negotiating competing stakeholder interests that can arise over the disposal of property. We have designated federal real property management as a high-risk area, in part because of the presence of underutilized properties.[1] As an alternative to increased agency use or disposal, some agencies initiated enhanced use lease (EUL) programs. EULs are typically long-term lease agreements that allow public or private entities to use the property.[2] Agency EUL programs have allowed entities to develop or occupy federal properties such as power plants, housing and healthcare facilities, office space, and parking facilities, and in return, federal agencies receive cash or in-kind consideration.[3] However, agencies also incur costs for EUL programs. We have previously reported that in any assessment of the cost/benefit of an agency's activities, all program costs should generally be included and any excluded costs should be disclosed and explained.[4] In 2011, we raised concerns about how the Department of Defense monitored the costs of its EUL program.[5] To help inform the discussion surrounding agencies' recent use of EULs to manage their federal real property portfolio, you asked us to examine issues related to these leases. Specifically, we addressed the following research questions:

1) To what extent do agencies attribute the full benefits and costs of their EULs in their assessments of their EUL programs?

2) What have been the experiences of agencies using their EUL authority?

To answer these questions, we reviewed prior GAO reports on enhanced-use leasing and capital financing[6] and identified agencies as candidates for a detailed review of EUL use.[7] To identify candidate agencies, we used Federal Real Property Profile data; the General Services Administration's (GSA) 2008 document *Real Property Authorities for Federal Agencies*; a prior GAO report on enhanced use leasing;[8] and interviews with officials at the four agencies that indicated they use EULs—the the Department of Veterans Affairs (VA), the National Aeronautics and Space Administration (NASA), the Department of State (State), and the Department of Agriculture (USDA). We reviewed relevant documentation related to these agencies' enhanced use leasing, including laws providing agencies with EUL authority, and agencies' EUL guidance. We also interviewed agency officials involved with developing and managing EULs. We chose a sample of 16 EULs from among the four agencies to review as case studies. We selected this sample to represent a variety of (1) lease purposes (e.g., leasing vacant land for development and leasing unused office space); (2) estimated financial benefits (e.g., cash benefits and in-kind consideration); and (3) geographic locations. We conducted site visits at nine of the 16 case study locations to observe the properties.[9] These site visits included NASA's Ames Research Center in Moffett Field, California; VA sites in Maryland, New Jersey, and Washington; and a USDA agricultural research center in Beltsville, Maryland. We interviewed agency officials and lessees about their experiences with EULs at these locations. In addition, we interviewed State officials about that department's EULs for properties located in Istanbul, Turkey; Paris, France; and Singapore. See appendix II for a list of case studies and descriptions of the properties and lessee uses. We reviewed the agreements between VA and its lessees and the past work of the Congressional Budget Office (CBO) and the VA's Office of Inspector General on VA's EULs in Chicago, Illinois; North Chicago, Illinois; and Mountain Home, Tennessee. We conducted interviews with officials from the Office of Management and Budget (OMB), CBO, and GSA to better understand government-wide views, guidance, and practices concerning EULs. See appendix I for more detailed information on our scope and methodology.

We conducted this performance audit from October 2011 to December 2012 in accordance with generally accepted government auditing standards. Those standards require that we plan and perform the audit to obtain sufficient, appropriate evidence to provide a reasonable basis for our findings and conclusions based on our audit objectives. We believe that the evidence obtained provides a reasonable basis for our findings and conclusions based on our audit objectives.

BACKGROUND

EULs are typically long-term leases of federal land or buildings to public sector or private sector companies. Some agencies with EUL authority are authorized to accept in-kind consideration, such as improvements to agency properties or construction of new facilities in place of cash rent. There is no government-wide definition of an enhanced use lease and agencies' EUL authorities and guidance vary, as these examples illustrate:

- VA was authorized to enter into EULs for up to 75 years with public and private entities for leases that contributed to VA's mission and would enhance the use of the property for cash or in-kind consideration; however, this authority expired on December 31, 2011. Prior to the expiration of VA's EUL authority, VA entered into 92 EULs that remain active. In August 2012, VA's EUL authority was reauthorized through December 2023, but the current authority allows VA to enter into EULs up to 75 years only for the provision of supportive housing for veterans or their families that are at risk of homelessness or are homeless. VA may accept cash consideration, or it may enter into an EUL without receiving consideration, and it is prohibited from entering into *leasebacks*.[10] VA may not enter into an EUL without advanced written certification from OMB that the lease complies with the statutory requirements.[11] VA reports annually on the details, benefits, and costs of its EUL program. The annual report states that it gives a transparent view of the measureable outcomes of the cost-effective benefits to veterans that the EUL program provides.
- NASA is authorized to enter into EULs of agency properties for cash consideration or, if the EULs involve the development of renewable energy production facilities, in-kind consideration.[12] NASA may not enter into leasebacks.[13] NASA policy requires that EULs relate to and

support the agency's mission of research, education, and exploration. The agency's longest EUL term is 95 years.[14] NASA's EUL authority expires in December 2017. NASA reports annually to Congress on its EUL program's status, proceeds, expenditures, and effectiveness.

- State is authorized to enter into EULs for its properties acquired in foreign countries for diplomatic and consular establishments.[15] State's longest EUL term is 99 years and expires in 2090. According to State officials, the agency does not have a formal EUL program. It has only utilized EULs in three instances. State uses EULs on a case by case basis when directed by Congress to retain properties or when it does not consider disposal a desirable option due to the strategic or historic value of an asset. For example, State was required to retain the Palazzo Corpi building in Istanbul, Turkey.[16] State carries the EULs in its property inventory and monitors the transactions and the cash flows but does not report externally on its EUL program.

- USDA is authorized to demonstrate whether enhanced use leasing of agency real property at its Beltsville Agricultural Research Center and the National Agricultural Library for cash consideration will enhance the use of the leased property.[17] The authority requires that EULs be consistent with the USDA's mission and have terms no longer than 30 years. USDA's EUL authority expires in June 2013. USDA reported to Congress on the management and performance measures associated with its EUL demonstration program and is required to report on the success of the program upon completion in 2013.

Table 1 shows how the four agencies we reviewed used EULs.

Table 1. General Description of EULs at Selected Agencies

Agency	General description of EULs
VA	EULs are located on VA sites throughout the nation and vary from individual buildings on VA campuses to entire VA campuses.
NASA	EULs are currently only located at the Ames Research Center in California and the Kennedy Space Center inFlorida, and are used for leasing space in existing buildings and leasing land for construction of buildings. The majority of NASA's EULs are located at the Ames Research Center in California.

Table 1. (Continued)

Agency	General description of EULs
State	EULs are for former U.S. diplomatic sites in France, Singapore, and Turkey.
USDA	Single EUL is limited to greenhouse space at a facility in Beltsville, Maryland.

Source: GAO analysis of agency data.

OMB coordinates and provides guidance on federal real property management government-wide in its role as Chair of the Federal Real Property Council, which is composed of federal real property-holding agencies. For example, OMB *Circular A-11* provides general guidance on evaluating the performance of federal programs and on the budgetary treatment of federal leases, including EULs and leaseback arrangements.[18] OMB's guidance does not provide specific information about the treatment of EULs, but does require EULs with leasebacks above certain threshold amounts be submitted to OMB for their budgetary-scoring impact. OMB's instructions also outline how budget authority for the cost of leasing an asset is to be recorded in the budget, depending on how risk is shared between the government and the lessee, for three types of leases: operating leases, capital leases, and lease purchases.[19]

AGENCIES ATTRIBUTED BENEFITS OF EULS TO THEIR EUL PROGRAMS, BUT DID NOT ALWAYS DO THE SAME WITH ALL COSTS

Agencies Cited Various EUL Benefits

Agency officials told us that EULs provide a variety of benefits to the government in addition to better utilization of underutilized federal property. The commonly cited benefits include enhanced mission activities, cash rent revenue, and value received through in-kind consideration.

Enhanced Mission Activities

Officials from the four agencies we reviewed said that EULs contribute to their ability to conduct mission-related activities; for example:

- VA officials said that EULs provide the agency mission-related benefits such as veterans' priority placement for housing. For example, according to VA, its EUL with Vancouver Housing Authority in Washington to develop a previously vacant site at a VA medical center campus supports the agency's strategic goals of (a) eliminating homelessness among veterans by providing housing and (b) reducing its inventory of vacant and underutilized capital assets.
- NASA officials said that EULs provide the agency mission-related benefits, such as research and development of aerospace technologies. For example, according to a NASA official, NASA's EUL with a company that researches and develops battery systems for electric vehicles advances the agency's mission of developing new power and propulsion systems for vehicles used in space launches.
- State officials said that EULs provide mission-related benefits by allowing the department to maintain properties symbolic of U.S. history and diplomacy. For example, State declared the historically significant Talleyrand building in Paris excess (see fig. 1) but chose not to dispose of it because the building had served as the administrative headquarters for the Marshall Plan, the postwar American reconstruction plan for Western Europe. According to State Department officials, State's EUL lessee supports the agency's mission by maintaining the building and retaining space inside of it for the George C. Marshall Center including a permanent exhibit commemorating the Marshall Plan.

Source: Department of State.

Figure 1. Department of State EUL for the Hôtel de Talleyrand in Paris, France.

- USDA officials said that the agency's EUL program allows it to better utilize property while also collaborating with researchers on mission-related goals. For example, USDA officials told us that its EUL of greenhouse space at its Beltsville Agricultural Research Center has allowed the agency to advance its mission of developing more efficient crops because the lessee conducts research at the EUL site directly linked to this goal. According to USDA officials, each EUL lessee is required to have a formal collaborative research agreement with the agency.

Cash Rent Revenue

All four agencies we reviewed reported cash benefits from EULs. Individual EULs can generate millions of dollars for the federal government, but most EULs generate small amounts of cash revenue. For example, the average VA EUL generated about $25,000 in cash revenue in fiscal year 2011.[20] See table 2 for the total cash rent revenue the four agencies in our review received in fiscal year 2011.

Table 2. Agencies' Reported Cash Rent Revenue from EULs, Fiscal Year 2011

Agency	Total cash rent revenue	Number of EULs
NASA	$8.0 million	71
State	$1.8 million	3
VA	$1.3 million	53
USDA	$15,569[a]	1

Source: GAO analysis of agency data.
[a] Rental income commenced May 20, 2011.

The following represents examples of the cash rent revenue that agencies received as part of EULs:

- NASA's most lucrative EUL is its lease for land on which its lessee plans to build office and research and development space for its employees. NASA receives about $3.66 million per year from this lessee. Over the 40-year lease, NASA expects to receive approximately $147.7 million in cash revenue.
- At one of its EULs, State received an up-front, one-time cash lump sum of $46 million and receives nominal annual cash rent payments

for the 99-year EUL of its former chief of mission residence and land in Singapore.[21] The lessee, a developer, constructed condominiums on the land (see fig. 2). Over the course of its 51-year lease for its Istanbul embassy property, State will receive approximately $20.6 million in cash revenue.

Source: Department of State.

Figure 2. **Department of State's** EUL for a Condominium Development in Singapore.

- VA received cash rental income of $340,000 in calendar year 2011 for its Somerville, New Jersey, EUL. The lessee renovated the warehouse and rented it to tenants.
- USDA received cash rental income of $15,569 in fiscal year 2011 for greenhouse space at its Beltsville Agricultural Research Center. The lessee uses the facility to research genetically modified plants.

In-Kind Consideration

VA, State, and NASA have also reported in-kind consideration as benefits of EULs. Specifically, VA estimated that it received in-kind consideration worth about $232 million from fiscal years 2006 through 2010. NASA estimated that it received in-kind consideration worth about $987,000 from fiscal years 2007 through 2011. State estimated that it received about $46 million in in-kind consideration from fiscal years 2008 through 2010. The specifics of in-kind arrangements with EUL lessees and the benefits claimed by agencies vary, for example:

- VA received priority placement for veterans in a housing facility built by the Vancouver Housing Authority as in-kind consideration in lieu of cash rent for its EUL in Vancouver, WA. VA officials said that this priority placement allowed VA to move patients from the hospital to transitional housing earlier, thus freeing up beds for other patients and reducing costs. (See fig. 3.) VA estimated the value of this priority placement at $2,866,327 in fiscal year 2011. At a different EUL site in Vancouver, WA, the Clark County government leased VA-owned land and constructed a four story community-health building on it. According to VA officials, in lieu of paying cash rent for the land, Clark County provided VA with approximately 23,000 square feet of free office space in the new building as in-kind consideration in fiscal year 2011. VA also received priority placement for veterans for all programs and services offered in the community-health building as in-kind consideration. VA estimated the total value of its in-kind consideration at $7,225,879 in fiscal year 2011. However, in 2012, the VA OIG found that VA often overstated the value of in-kind consideration in its annual report on the performance of its EUL program.[22] According to VA officials, VA is recalculating and updating its EUL methodology used to report expenses and benefits. VA officials stated that, as required by law, the revised EUL lease consideration calculations will be reported in VA's fiscal year 2014 budget that the agency plans to release in February 2013.[23]

Source: GAO.

Figure 3. Housing Facility Located on Property that VA Leases to the Vancouver Housing Authority in Vancouver, Washington.

- A NASA EUL lessee at the Ames Research Center made improvements, such as investments in fire protection and electrical systems, to the facility the lessee rents as in-kind consideration in lieu of some of a cash-rent requirement to NASA. NASA estimated the total value of this in-kind consideration to be $586,044 from 2004 through 2009. One of NASA's EULs includes a provision for in-kind consideration of about $1 million if the lessee built a new water tower, park, and security gate under certain time frames.[24]
- State's EUL with a lessee for the Talleyrand building in Paris also included in-kind consideration. In exchange for reduced cash rent of $46 million, the lessee renovated the entire building including space to house the Department of State's George C. Marshall Center.

Some Agencies Do Not Attribute All Costs of EULs to Their EUL Programs in a Consistent, Appropriate Manner

Some of the agencies we reviewed do not include all costs associated with their EULs when they assess the performance of their EUL programs. Federal agencies are required to assess and report the full costs of their activities to provide relevant and reliable cost information to assist the Congress and federal executives in making decisions about allocating federal resources, assessing costs and benefits to compare alternative courses of action, authorizing and modifying programs, and evaluating program performance.[25] However, OMB *Circular A-11* guidance is broad and does not specify what costs agencies should attribute to their EUL programs, resulting in variance among agencies. Without fully accounting for all EUL costs, agencies may overstate the net benefits of their EUL programs. Specifically, we noted variances in whether agencies attributed consultant costs, termination costs, and leaseback costs to their overall EUL program costs.

Consultant Costs

NASA and USDA attribute consultant costs to their EUL programs, but VA and State do not. Agencies use consultants to provide subject matter expertise and technical support for their EULs, such as conducting real estate appraisals, market analyses, engineering studies, and general consulting services.

- According to NASA officials, the agency spent about $2 million on consultants to support its EUL program from fiscal years 2006 to 2011. Agency officials added that these costs are attributed to NASA's total EUL program costs in NASA's annual budget reports to provide a fully transparent accounting of the net benefits of the program.

- According to USDA officials, the agency incurred one consultant fee as part of its EUL program—a $10,250 market appraisal to determine rental rates for properties selected for the program. USDA officials said that the agency attributed the consultant costs to its EUL program and plans to include all costs, including consultant costs, in its final report at the conclusion of the agency's EUL demonstration program.

- According to VA officials, consultants are generally realty specialists who provide support throughout the various stages of executing an EUL agreement. In addition to supplying real estate expertise, EUL consultants may facilitate obtaining various reports that are generated as part of VA's due diligence on EUL projects. Such reports can include environmental site assessments, property appraisals, surveys of EUL parcels, title searches, and various other documentation required by law. In fiscal years 2006 to 2011, the agency awarded approximately $28 million to consultants related specifically to the formulation or support of the agency's EULs. We reviewed VA's consultant costs related to its EUL program and found that VA had not attributed any consultant costs to the EUL program.

- State's consultant fees for developing, implementing, and overseeing its EULs in Paris and Istanbul were approximately $723,000 from fiscal years 2006 to 2011. State was unable to verify expenses for developing and implementing its EUL in Singapore because of the age of the project.[26] State does not attribute the costs of consultant fees to its EUL program costs. State officials said that they do not have any consultants with sole EUL responsibility and they consider consultant fees to be under the category of administrative costs. State officials noted that the amount of consultant fees specifically related to EULs is a negligible part of the agency's overall consultant fees because EULs represent a very small portion of State's 20,000 properties worldwide.

Cost of Terminating EULs

VA and NASA have incurred costs related to terminating EULs that they did not attribute to their EUL programs. Costs that result from terminating EULs prior to the end of the term are important considerations for decision makers when determining if EULs are viable and beneficial to the agency. VA has terminated seven EULs since 1991. According to VA, in most cases, the agency terminated the lease because either the lessee did not fulfill the terms and conditions of the lease or the lease was mutually terminated. Most recently, VA terminated an EUL, and according to VA officials, the cost as of fiscal year 2011 associated with terminating this lease was $287,000 for ongoing litigation. We reviewed VA's termination costs and found that VA had not attributed termination costs to its EUL program. VA officials said that they do not attribute costs associated with termination to its total EUL program costs because it attributes these costs at a higher budgetary level.

According to NASA, the Ames Research Center has terminated 11 EULs since 2003, which NASA officials told us were mostly short duration leases for office space and included three EULs that were terminated for the purpose of consolidating them into one new lease with the same lessee. NASA officials said that some termination costs, such as time spent calculating a lessee's penalty for terminating a lease, are not attributed to EUL program costs. NASA officials told us that these costs have been minimal and cannot be tracked to either EULs or activities related to terminating leases and are instead considered general administrative costs.

Leaseback Costs

Among the four agencies we reviewed, only VA currently leases back space or services from its EUL lessees. In fiscal year 2011, VA leased back some or all of its space at seven of its EUL sites at a cost of about $15.8 million. For example, VA received $340,000 in rent for its EUL in Somerville, New Jersey, but at the same time paid approximately $181,000 to lease back part of the facility.[27] According to VA, the agency received the use of one loading bay rent free as in-kind consideration and paid approximately $15,000 for utilities, operations, and maintenance related to that bay. Two years later, VA requested a second bay in the facility for which, according to VA, it paid approximately $166,000 in rent. The agency did not consider any of the leaseback costs as arising as part of the EUL transaction and instead claimed the entire $340,000 in rental income as the cash benefit of the EUL.

The appropriate treatment of leaseback costs in determining the net benefit of an EUL is an area that may require further clarification in OMB guidance. It is unclear, for example, whether leaseback costs associated with VA's leaseback arrangements should be taken into account in determining the net benefit of the EUL's rental income. On the one hand, the $181,000 paid for the leaseback as described above could be viewed as an effective reduction in the lease payment from the lessee. On the other hand, in the absence of the EUL, it is possible that VA would have expended funds to obtain these warehousing facilities in some other way. It may thus not represent net additional cost to VA and it may not be appropriate to view the leaseback as having effectively reduced the rental income of the EUL.

AGENCIES' EXPERIENCES IN USING EULs PROVIDE ILLUSTRATIVE EXAMPLES ABOUT EUL USE

Based on recent agency experiences, EULs may be a viable option for redeveloping underutilized federal real property when disposal is not possible or desirable, but agencies raised issues pertaining to EULs that affect their use or budgetary treatment. First, NASA has reported that the limitation on its authority to accept in-kind consideration has limited its ability to encourage use of EULs and investments in underutilized NASA property. Second, recognizing potential budget impacts associated with EUL leasebacks and other long-term commitments has proved challenging for VA. Although the results of our review cannot be generalized to all agencies, these challenges provide illustrative examples of the types of issues that can affect a federal agency's decision or ability to use EULs.

In-Kind Consideration

According to NASA officials, in-kind consideration is critical for encouraging lessees to invest in agency properties. NASA's ability to accept in-kind consideration expired at the end of 2008; it was restored on a limited basis in 2011 exclusively for renewable energy projects. NASA officials said that this limitation in the agency's ability to accept in-kind consideration has hindered its ability to enter into EULs that could improve the property. In particular, according to the NASA officials, prospective lessees are reluctant to make capital improvements that will have to be conveyed to the government at the end of the lease without receiving other compensation, such as a reduction in cash rent. For example, a lessee, as previously discussed, agreed to invest $11 million in infrastructure projects that would benefit the company during the lease but benefit the government during and after the lease in return for a reduction in the lessee's cash rent payments. Representatives from NASA and the lessee told us that this provision was critical to successfully negotiating the EUL.

Budget Impacts of EULs

VA officials said that assessing and recognizing the budget impacts of EULs is complicated and maybe interpreted differently by agencies with EUL authority. In particular, VA EULs can include long-term commitments that are recognized in the federal budget in different ways. OMB's *Circular* No. A-11 guidance specifies that lease obligations be recorded when the contract is signed; sufficient budget authority must be available at that time to cover the obligation. However, the obligated amount that is to be recorded differs by type of lease. For capital leases and lease purchases, OMB *Circular A-11* states that the amount obligated should equal the net present value of these lease payments over the full term of the lease. For operating leases, OMB *Circular A-11* states that agencies should record an amount equal to the total payments under the full term of the lease or the first year's lease payments plus cancellation costs.[28] VA views EUL leasebacks as operating leases and consequently does not obligate the total amount of these commitments upfront in its budget. VA's leaseback costs are nearly $16 million annually (see table 3), but VA and CBO disagree on the extent to which VA should account for the budget impacts for EULs that could include long-term government commitments. For example, VA's leaseback costs for its Chicago West Side EUL were about $3.5 million in fiscal year 2011. VA regards its underlying office and parking purchase agreements as 2-year operating leases, as opposed to capital leases or lease purchases. VA officials said that the department is properly treating the office and parking purchase agreements as operating leases, because VA can cancel the office and parking leasebacks at the end of each 2-year agreement. However, in a 2003 report to Congress on the budgetary treatment of leases, CBO found that VA used this enhanced use lease to obtain a $60 million regional headquarters building and parking facility. The CBO report stated that VA entered into a 35-year enhanced use lease for a four-acre site with an owner trust, with VA as the sole named beneficiary. VA subsequently leased back space in the building and the parking facility that the lessee constructed on the site.

The CBO report also stated that:

- VA's lease payments played a crucial role in allowing the lessee to borrow funds. VA is committed to a two-year lease of 95 percent of the space in the building and 95 percent of the parking facility; almost all of the lessee's revenue will initially come from VA.
- The initial two-year lease is automatically renewed unless the VA takes specific steps at the end of the lease period to halt it. In addition, as long as VA chooses to occupy any portion of the facility it must make payments that are sufficient to cover amortization and interest on the lessee's debt.
- VA also has the right to purchase the building from the lessee at any time for a price that would cover payments on the lessee's debt.
- Thus, VA has a long-term commitment to cover the lessee's capital costs even if it reduces its occupancy in the building, and this, together with an implicit right to renew the lease, would appear to make the arrangement either a lease-purchase or, if the trust is not viewed as a separate entity from VA, a government purchase financed by federal borrowing.

As such, CBO concluded in its report that the intent of the West Side EUL project was to provide VA with capital assets (an office building and parking facilities for VA staff) without recording the cost of the purchase upfront in the budget.[29] In general, we have also consistently stated that the full costs of the government's commitments should be reflected upfront in the budget.[30] In commenting on a draft of this report, VA officials said the agency made changes in subsequent EULs to address and in their view eliminate CBO's early concerns related to EULs with leasebacks.

Table 3. VA EUL Leaseback Costs in Fiscal Year 2011

EUL location	Type of EUL project	VA leaseback costs,fiscal year 2011
Leavenworth, KS	Residential health care	$14,989[a]
Milwaukee, WI	Office space for VA regional staff	$2,448,713
Somerville, NJ	Mixed use warehouse	$181,391

EUL location	Type of EUL project	VA leaseback costs, fiscal year 2011
Salt Lake City I, UT	Office space for VA regional and field staff	$2,142,451
Salt Lake City II, UT	Office space for VA regional and field staff	$2,626,209
Chicago (WestSide), IL	Office space for VA regional staff	$3,502,894
Atlanta, GA	Office space for VA regional staff	$4,910,903
Total		$15,827,550

Source: GAO analysis of VA data.

[a]According to VA, the building was not operational until April 2011, therefore this is not a full year payment.

VA also has energy project EULs at Chicago West Side, Illinois; North Chicago, Illinois; and Mountain Home, Tennessee, which have a similar legal structure as the Chicago West Side agreement for the regional headquarters building. VA officials stated that they disagree with CBO's conclusions about the budget impacts of these EULs. VA entered into 35- year EULs for land with owner trusts as part of the energy project EULs. In return the lessee agrees to build power plants to service on-site VA facilities. VA purchases power from the plants at a fixed price,[31] in lieu of GSA energy utility contracts, for stipulated two-year terms, subject to certain anticipated renewal provisions. VA is committed to purchase power from the lessee at fixed prices as long as the VA center remained open and even if VA reduced its level of purchases, VA would continue to cover the lessee's capital costs. These purchase agreements with VA provided enough security to allow the lessees to obtain private loans to construct the power plants. VA officials said that VA did not report the total 35-year commitment for these EULs in its budget because of its determination that the cost to provide energy services to VA medical centers is not a new expenditure and without the EUL—VA would still need to procure services to power medical centers. In addition, VA officials said that they believe that accounting for all 35 years of costs upfront in the budget would not be technically appropriate, since VA would be determining in advance that it would prospectively receive energy under the purchase agreements for 35 year periods without recognizing VA's two-year renewal options. However, CBO reported that VA's commitment to pay the lessees annual amounts sufficient to service the private debt on the power plants—regardless of whether VA uses the power produced—as constituting a legally binding obligation of the federal government that should be recorded in full upfront in the budget.[32]

CONCLUSION

Agencies have shown that EULs have the potential to produce mission-related and financial benefits for otherwise underutilized federal real property, but the costs and benefits of these programs are not fully understood, given different agency practices in accounting for EUL costs. Some EULs bring in large amounts of cash rent, such as the State Department's $20.6 million Istanbul EUL and NASA's $147.7 million EUL, but most EULs have much more modest benefits to the government where the costs could more easily outweigh the benefits. For example, the average VA EUL earned about $25,000 in cash revenue last year— financial benefits that could be outweighed by consultant, termination, and leaseback costs, which agencies have not consistently attributed to their EUL programs. Lacking clear guidance and failing to incorporate all of the costs related to agencies' EUL programs could cause agencies to overstate the net benefits of these programs when reporting the performance of their EUL programs or making decisions about future EULs.

RECOMMENDATION

To promote transparency about EULs, improve decision-making regarding EULs, and ensure more accurate accounting of EUL net benefits, we recommend that OMB work with VA, NASA, State, and USDA, and any other agencies with EUL authority, to ensure that agencies consistently attribute all costs associated with EULs (such as consulting, termination, and leaseback costs) to their EUL programs, as appropriate.

AGENCY COMMENTS

We provided a draft of this report to the Deputy Director for Management of OMB and the Secretaries of Veterans Affairs, State, and Agriculture and the

Administrator of NASA for review and comment. In commenting on a draft of this report, OMB generally agreed with GAO's observations and recommendation. OMB emphasized that *Circular No. A-11* provides guidance on budget scoring and is not intended to address the costs and benefits of EULs. We amended our recommendation to reflect that there are a variety of ways to ensure that the costs of EULs are consistently tracked and reported. Veterans Affairs, State, Agriculture, and NASA generally agreed with our conclusions and the agencies provided technical comments, which we incorporated as appropriate.

Sincerely yours,

David J. Wise
Director
Physical Infrastructure Issues

APPENDIX I: OBJECTIVES, SCOPE, AND METHODOLOGY

Our objectives were to determine:

1) To what extent do agencies attribute the full benefits and costs of their EULs in their assessments of their EUL programs?
2) What have been the experiences of agencies in using their EUL authority?

To address these both of these objectives we reviewed prior GAO reports on enhanced use leasing and capital financing,[1] and contacted the Office of Management and Budget (OMB), Congressional Budget Office (CBO) and 11 agencies: (1) Veterans Affairs (VA), (2) National Aeronautics and Space Administration (NASA), (3) Department of State (State), (4) Department of Agriculture (USDA), (5) General Services Administration (GSA), (6) Department of Energy (Energy), (7) Department of Interior (Interior), (8) Department of Justice (DOJ), (9) United States Postal Service (USPS), (10) St. Lawrence Seaway Development Corporation (SLSDC), and (11) Tennessee Valley Authority (TVA) based on size or evidence of EUL authority.[2] We identified the 11 agencies based on our review of property data and documents from: (1) The 7 largest civilian real property holding agencies, by total square footage, as of fiscal year 2010, as listed in the Federal Real Property Profile,[3]

(2) GSA's Real Property Authorities for Federal Agencies (2008), (3) *Agencies' Authorities Regarding EULs and Real Property Sales* from GAO-09-283R, and (4) interviews with officials from agencies identified in the above 3 sources to determine if they used EULs and if they knew of any other agencies that used EULs. Using information from the 11 agencies we contacted, we selected the 4 agencies (VA, NASA, State and USDA) that have used their EUL authority to enter into EULs.[4] We selected 16 case study EULs from the four agencies that have EULs based on a range of lease purposes (e.g., leasing of vacant land for development and leasing unused office space); estimated financial benefits (e.g., cash benefits and in-kind consideration); and varying geographic locations. The case studies were located in Chicago, IL; North Chicago, IL; Mountain Home, TN; Vancouver, WA; Somerville, NJ; Moffett Field, CA; Beltsville, MD; Fort Howard, MD; Paris, France; Istanbul, Turkey, and Singapore. Because the 16 case studies were selected based on a non-probability sample, observations made based on our review of the 16 case study locations do not support generalizations about other EUL sites. Rather, the observations made provided specific, detailed examples of issues that were described by agency officials and lessees. We also interviewed agency officials at the local level and headquarters locations, and reviewed relevant laws describing agencies' EUL authorities and agency documentation, including agencies' regulations and guidance on enhanced use leasing. We visited the 9 case studies located in the U.S. to observe the properties firsthand, interviewed agency officials and lessees about their experience with EULs at these locations, and reviewed documentation regarding these properties. The case study EULs were located at NASA's Ames Research Center in Moffett Field, California, VA sites in Maryland, New Jersey and Washington state, and a USDA agricultural research center in Beltsville, Maryland. For the three State case studies we did not visit, we interviewed headquarters officials and reviewed relevant documentation including site-visit reports. For the four VA sites we did not visit in Chicago, Illinois, Chicago (West Side), Illinois; North Chicago, Illinois; and Mountain Home, Tennessee, we reviewed the agreements between VA and its lessees and the past work of the Congressional Budget Office and the VA's Office of Inspector General. We also interviewed OMB, CBO, and GSA officials to better understand government-wide views, guidance, and practices on enhanced use leasing.

We conducted this performance audit from October 2011 to December 2012 in accordance with generally accepted government auditing standards. Those standards require that we plan and perform the audit to obtain sufficient, appropriate evidence to provide a reasonable basis for our findings and conclusions based on our audit objectives. We believe that the evidence obtained provides a reasonable basis for our findings and conclusions based on our audit objectives.

APPENDIX II: 16 CASE STUDY ENHANCED USE LEASES BY LOCATION, PROPERTY TYPE, AND TENANT USE

As shown in table 3, we reviewed 16 case study EULs. We reviewed 8 VA EULs, 4 from NASA, 3 from State, and 1 from USDA.

Table 4. EULs by Agency

Agency	Location	Agency property	EUL tenant use of property
VA	Somerville, NJ	Warehouse	Renovate warehouse
	Vancouver, WA	Vacant land	Construct health care facility
	Vancouver, WA	Vacant land	Construct housing
	Fort Howard, MD	Vacant land and buildings	Construct housing
	Chicago, IL (WestSide)	Vacant land	Construct office space and parking facility
	Chicago, IL	Vacant land	Construct energy center
	Mountain Home, TN	Vacant land	Construct co-generation plant
	North Chicago, IL	Vacant land	Construct energy center
NASA	Moffett Field, CA	Animal research facility	Animal husbandry and research
	Moffett Field, CA	Warehouse	Electric vehicle research
	Moffett Field, CA	Vacant land	Construct multi-story office buildings and researchand development space
	Moffett Field, CA	Hangar	Storage of satellite equipment
State	Istanbul, Turkey	Historic embassy compound	Restore and convert buildings, construct hotel
	Paris, France	Historically significant building	Restore building and lease office space
	Singapore	Embassy property	Build condominiums
USDA	Beltsville, MD	Greenhouse	Plant-based research

Source: GAO analysis of agency data.

End Notes

[1] GAO, *High-Risk Series: An Update*, GAO-11-278 (Washington, D.C.: February 2011).

[2] There is no government-wide definition of EULs. This definition was drawn from GAO, *Federal Real Property: Authorities and Actions Regarding Enhanced Use Leases and Sale of Unneeded Real Property*, GAO-09-283R (Washington, D.C.: Feb. 17, 2009).

[3] In-kind consideration refers to goods or services that a lessee provides to an agency in lieu of cash rent payments.

[4] GAO, *GAO Cost Estimating and Assessment Guide: Best Practices for Developing and Managing Capital Program Costs*, GAO-09-3SP (Washington, D.C.: March 2009).

[5] GAO, *Defense Infrastructure: The Enhanced Use Lease Program Requires Management Attention*, GAO-11-574, (Washington, D.C.: June 30, 2011).

[6] GAO, GAO-11-574; GAO, *NASA: Enhanced Use Leasing Program Needs Additional Controls*, GAO-07-306R (Washington, D.C.: Mar. 1, 2007); and GAO, *Capital Financing: Partnerships and Energy Savings Performance Contracts Raise Budgeting and Monitoring Concerns*, GAO-05-55 (Washington, D.C.: Dec., 16, 2004).

[7] We excluded the Department of Defense (DOD) because GAO recently issued a report on DOD's EUL program, see GAO-11-574.

[8] GAO-09-283R.

[9] Because this is a nonprobability sample, observations made based on our review of the 16 case study locations do not support generalizations about other EUL sites. Rather, the observations made provided specific, detailed examples of issues that were described by agency officials and lessees.

[10] A *leaseback* is an arrangement in which an agency leases an asset to another entity, then leases back services or property from the lessee. For example, an agency may lease a warehouse facility to the private sector and then rent back some space for its own use.

[11] 38 U.S.C. § 8162.

[12] 51 U.S.C. § 20145(b).

[13] 51 U.S.C. § 20145(e)(1).

[14] According to NASA officials, the total potential term of this lease is 95 years, comprised of a 5-year initial term, a primary term of 60 years, and lessee's right to three unilateral extensions of 10 years each.

[15] 22 U.S.C. § 300.

[16] Pub. L. No. 108-199, § 633(e) (Jan. 23, 2004).

[17] 7 U.S.C. § 3125a note.

[18] OMB, *Circular A-11 Preparation, Submission, and Execution of the Budget* (August 2012).

[19] Operating leases are defined in OMB *Circular* No. A-11 as meeting the following criteria: (1) Ownership of the asset remains with the lessor during the term of the lease and is not transferred to the government at or shortly after the end of the lease term; (2) the lease does not contain a bargain-price purchase option; (3) the lease term does not exceed 75 percent of the estimated economic life of the asset; (4) the present value of the minimum lease payments over the life of the lease does not exceed 90 percent of the fair market value of the asset at the beginning of the lease term; (5) the asset is a general-purpose asset rather than being for a special purpose of the government and is not built to the unique specification of the government as lessee; and (6) there is a private sector market for the asset. A capital lease is any lease other than a lease-purchase that does not meet the criteria of an operating lease. Lease-purchase means a type of lease in which ownership of the asset is transferred to

the government at or shortly after the end of the lease term. Such a lease may or may not contain a bargain-price purchase option.

[20] While most of VA's EULs did not generate cash revenue in fiscal year 2011, among the 17 of 53 VA EULs that generated cash revenue, the average was about $79,000 per EUL.

[21] According to State officials, the agency receives an annual nominal rent payment of $1,000 Singapore dollars (or about $760 U.S. dollars), a payment that is a common practice for long-term, prepaid leases.

[22] VA Office of Inspector General, Department of Veterans Affairs, *Audit of the Enhanced-Use Lease Program* (Feb. 19, 2012).

[23] Each year as part of the annual budget submission of the President to Congress, the VA Secretary is required to submit a detailed report of the consideration received for each enhanced use lease, along with an overview of how VA is using such consideration to support veterans. *See* 38 U.S.C. § 8168(b).

[24] According to NASA, the lessee did not complete the projects by the required deadlines and therefore had to repay NASA the cash value of in-kind consideration already provided to the agency (approximately $890,000); however, per the terms of the EUL, the lessee is still required to construct the infrastructure, share it with the agency, and convey it to the government upon completion of the infrastructure improvements.

[25] Federal Accounting Standards Advisory Board, *Statement of Federal Financial Accounting Standards 4: Managerial Cost Accounting Standards and Concepts*, Pronouncements as Amended, Version 7 (June 2008).

[26] State officials said because the Singapore EUL was awarded in 1991, they no longer had information on expenses.

[27] VA received the $340,000 payment for calendar year 2011 and paid for the warehouse space it used for fiscal year 2011.

[28] For prior GAO reports on the budgetary treatment of federal leases; see, for example, GAO-05-55; GAO, Budget Issues: *Alternative Approaches to Finance Federal Capital*, GAO-03-1011 (Washington, D.C.: Aug. 21, 2003); and GAO, Federal Real Property: *NIH Has Improved Its Leasing Process, but Needs to Provide Congress with Information on Some Leases*, GAO-06-918 (Washington, D.C.: Sept. 8, 2006).

[29] Congressional Budget Office, *The Budgetary Treatment of Leases and Public/Private Ventures*, (Washington, D.C.: February 2003) at 33-34 and 45.

[30] See GAO-05-55, GAO-03-1011, and GAO-06-918.

[31] For both Chicago EULs, if the established rates for power are at least 25 percent higher than available market rates, the rates will be renegotiated.

[32] See Congressional Budget Office, *The Budgetary Treatment of Leases and Public/Private Venture* (Washington, D.C.: February 2003).

End Notes for Appendix I

[1] GAO, *Defense Infrastructure: The Enhanced Use Lease Program Requires Management Attention*, GAO-11-574, (Washington, D.C.: June 30, 2011); GAO, *Federal Real Property: Authorities and Actions Regarding Enhanced Use Leases and Sale of Unneeded Real Property*, GAO-09-283R (Washington, D.C.: Feb. 17, 2009); GAO, *NASA: Enhanced Use Leasing Program Needs Additional Controls*, GAO-07-306R (Washington, D.C.: Mar. 1, 2007); and GAO, *Capital Financing: Partnerships and Energy Savings Performance*

Contracts Raise Budgeting and Monitoring Concerns, GAO-05-55, (Washington, D.C.: December 16, 2004).

[2] We excluded the Department of Defense (DOD) because GAO recently issued a report on DOD's EUL program, see GAO-11-574.

[3] We reported on problems with the FRPP data in GAO, *Federal Real Property: National Strategy and Better Data Needed to Improve Management of Excess and Underutilized Property,* GAO-12-645, (Washington, D.C. June 20, 2012), but determined that it was suitable for purposes of this report.

[4] We excluded several of these agencies because they did not have EULs or EUL authority (Interior, Justice, and the St. Lawrence Seaway Development Corporation). GSA has EUL authority, but has not awarded EULs. Further, USPS and Tennessee Valley Authority officials told us that they do not consider their leases or leasebacks, respectively, as EULs. We also excluded DOD because we recently issued a report on its EUL program, GAO-11-574.

In: Federal Real Property Management   ISBN: 978-1-63321-219-0
Editor: Aaron F. Darby   © 2014 Nova Science Publishers, Inc.

Chapter 4

FEDERAL REAL PROPERTY: AUTHORITIES AND ACTIONS REGARDING ENHANCED USE LEASES AND SALE OF UNNEEDED REAL PROPERTY[*]

United States Government Accountability Office

The Honorable Edolphus Towns
Chairman
Committee on Oversight and Government Reform
House of Representatives

The Honorable Darrell Issa
Ranking Member
Committee on Oversight and Government Reform
House of Representatives

Many federal agencies hold real property that they do not need, including property that is underutilized or excess.[1] Such properties present significant potential risks to federal agencies because they are costly to maintain and could be put to more cost-beneficial uses or sold to generate revenue for the

---

[*] This is an edited, reformatted and augmented version of a U.S. Government Accountability Office report, GAO-09-283R, dated February 17, 2009.

government. We first designated federal real property management as a high-risk area in January 2003 due to longstanding problems with underutilized and excess property, among other things.[2] After our high-risk designation, President George W. Bush added real property management to the President's Management Agenda and directed that the Federal Real Property Profile (FRPP) be established as a comprehensive database of real property under the control and custody of executive branch agencies, with agencies required to report on their real property assets each year.[3] The President also established a goal of disposing of $15 billion in unneeded real property assets by 2015 to encourage agencies to right-size their portfolios by eliminating unneeded property.

Some federal agencies have been granted authorities to enter into enhanced use leases (EUL)—typically long-term agreements with public and private entities for the use of federal property, resulting in cash and/or in-kind consideration for the agency—or to retain the proceeds from the sale of real property. Given the large number of unneeded properties being held by the federal government, you asked that we review how agencies are using their disposal authorities. Therefore, we addressed (1) what authorities the 10 largest real property holding agencies have to enter into EULs and retain proceeds from the sale of real property; (2) the extent to which agencies with authority to retain proceeds sold real property and how they have used the proceeds; and (3) the relationship, if any, between agencies having the authority to enter into EULs or retain sales proceeds and the amount of real property that they retained or sold.

To address these questions, we analyzed agencies' legal authorities related to EULs and the sale and retention of proceeds of real property; analyzed agency real property and FRPP data; and gathered, analyzed, and synthesized documentary and testimonial evidence of the 10 largest real property holding federal agencies (by value of real property). These 10 agencies include the Department of Agriculture (USDA), Department of Defense (DOD), Department of Energy (DOE), Department of the Interior (DOI), Department of Justice (DOJ), Department of State (State), Department of Veterans Affairs (VA), General Services Administration (GSA), National Aeronautics and Space Administration (NASA), and the United States Postal Service (USPS). For the purposes of this review, the term "real property" does not include real property that DOD has or is planning to dispose of through the Base Realignment and Closure Act (BRAC) process,[4] lands managed by DOI or the Forest Service (except for Forest Service administrative sites), and transfers of individual properties specifically authorized by Congress. We also conducted site visits of real property that agencies have recently sold, exchanged, or were attempting to sell, and a property being leased under an EUL agreement and collected data from agencies on their real property sales during fiscal years 2006 and 2007. (See encl. I for additional information on our scope and methodology.)

We conducted our work in Arlington, Va.; Camp Verde, Ariz.; Colorado Springs, Colo.; Denver; Estes Park, Colo.; Glendale, Ariz.; Guilderland, N.Y.; Hillsborough, N.J.; Loveland, Colo.; Middle River, Md.; New York City; Peoria, Ariz.; Rotterdam, N.Y.; Scotia, N.Y.; Scottsdale, Ariz.; Sedona, Ariz.; Tucson, Ariz.; and Washington, D.C., from April 2008 through February 2009.

RESULTS IN BRIEF

The 10 largest real property holding agencies have different authorities regarding EULs and retention of proceeds from the sale of real property. As of the end of fiscal year 2008,

- six agencies had both the authority to enter into EULs and sell and retain the proceeds from the sale of real property (DOD, GSA, State, USDA's Forest Service, USPS, and VA);
- two agencies had EUL authority but no authority to retain proceeds from the sale of real property (DOE and NASA); and
- three agencies had no authority either to enter into EULs or retain proceeds from the sale of real property (USDA,[5] excluding the Forest Service; DOI;[6] and DOJ).

Authorities are agency-specific and include different provisions. For example, while VA is authorized to enter into EULs for "underutilized" or "unutilized" real property, DOD is authorized to enter into EULs only for "nonexcess" real property. In addition, while DOD, GSA, and VA have the authority to retain proceeds from the sale of real property, DOD (in some cases), GSA, and VA are required to follow several steps before possibly selling the property, including offering it to other federal agencies, eligible organizations that will use the property to assist the homeless, and other public benefit purposes. However, the Forest Service, State, and USPS sell real property and retain the proceeds without following these additional steps. Moreover, four agencies have the authority to retain proceeds from the sale of real property and use them without further congressional action (DOD in certain cases, the Forest Service, State,[7] and USPS) while further congressional action is required before two agencies (VA for nonEUL property[8] and GSA) may use the proceeds.

The six agencies with authority to retain proceeds reported selling property to varying extents and using proceeds primarily to help manage their real property portfolios. Governmentwide data reported to the FRPP were not sufficiently reliable to quantify the extent to which these agencies sold real property. As a result, we were unable to use the FRPP to analyze the number of sales of real property by agencies with the authority to retain proceeds. However, the six agencies we contacted that have authority to retain proceeds from the sale of real property provided data on their net proceeds from the sale of real property during fiscal years 2006 and 2007, which ranged from $21 million to $541 million per agency. While some properties sold for tens of thousands of dollars, others sold for over $200 million. Agencies generally reported using the sales proceeds to manage their real property portfolios, such as rental of space, building operations, new construction and acquisition, maintenance, and repairs and operations.

Agency officials generally said that the authorities to enter into EULs and sell real property and retain the proceeds influenced the amount of property that is kept and sold and that they preferred using the authorities that were the least restrictive. Because we were unable to quantify the number of properties that agencies sold during fiscal years 2006 and 2007, we asked agency officials about their views on the relationship between having the authorities to enter into EULs or retain sales proceeds and the amount of real property that they sell. Of the six agencies with the authority to retain proceeds from the sale of real property, officials at five agencies (the Forest Service, GSA, State, USPS, and VA) said that this authority is a strong incentive to sell real property, while officials at DOD said that the authority to retain proceeds is not a strong incentive to sell real property. Agencies with both authorities—to enter into EULs and retain proceeds from the sale of real property— prefer using the authority with the fewest restrictions. For example, VA indicated that EUL authority allows the agency to manage unneeded property because (1) VA may enter into EUL agreements without following steps required to sell real property, such as screening the property for use by the homeless, and (2) VA has the authority to retain and spend proceeds generated from EULs without the need for further congressional action. On the other hand, officials at USPS said that USPS has little incentive to enter into EULs and instead focuses on selling or exchanging property to maximize benefits to its real estate portfolio. The five agencies that do not have the authority to retain proceeds from the sale of real property (DOE; DOI; DOJ; NASA; and USDA except for the Forest Service), provided mixed responses about the extent to which such an authority would be an incentive to sell unneeded real property. While officials at all five agencies said that they would like to have such expanded authorities to help manage their real property portfolios, officials at two of those agencies said that due to challenges such as the security needs or remote locations of most of their properties, it was unlikely that they would sell many properties.

We requested comments on a draft of this report from the 10 real property holding agencies in our review and OMB. DOE, GSA, and DOI agreed with the information presented in the report. DOE, GSA, NASA, OMB, State, USDA, and VA provided technical clarifications, which we incorporated throughout the report as appropriate. The other agencies did not provide comments.

AGENCIES HAVE DIFFERENT AUTHORITIES REGARDING EULS AND RETENTION OF PROCEEDS FROM SALE OF REAL PROPERTY

Separate legislation has provided agencies with their own statutory authorities regarding EULs and retaining proceeds from the sale of real property. The 10 largest real property holding agencies have different authorities for EULs and retention of proceeds from the sale of real property. As of the end of fiscal year 2008, eight agencies had the authority to enter into EULs (DOD, DOE, GSA, NASA, State, USDA's Forest Service, USPS, and VA) and six agencies (DOD, the Forest Service, GSA, State, USPS, and VA) had the authority to sell and retain proceeds from the sale of real property. Six agencies had both authorities to enter into EULs and to retain proceeds from the sale of real property (DOD, GSA, State, USDA's Forest Service, USPS, and VA); two agencies had EUL authority but no authority to retain proceeds from the sale of real property (DOE and NASA); and three agencies had no authority to enter into EULs or retain proceeds from the sale of real property (USDA, excluding the Forest Service; DOI; and DOJ).[9] The authorities of these agencies are shown in table 1. For more information on agencies' legal authorities related to real property EULs, sales, and retention of proceeds, see enclosure II.

Table 1. Agencies' Authorities Regarding EULs and Real Property Sales

Agency	Authority to enter into EULs and retain leasing proceeds	Authority to use proceeds from EULs without further congressional action	Authority to sell real property and retain sales proceeds	Authority to use proceeds from sales without further congressional action
DOD	X	X	X	X[a]
DOE	Xb			
GSA	X		X	
DOIc				
DOJ				
NASA	X	X		
State[d]	X	X	X	X[e]
USDA (except the Agricultural Research Service[f] and the Forest Service)				
USDA (Forest Service)[g]	X[h]	X	X	X
USPS	X	X	X	X
VA	X	X	X	[i]

Source: GAO analysis and information provided by the above agencies. Note: Authorities through fiscal year 2008.

[a] In certain cases, the use of proceeds from the sale of DOD real property is subject to further congressional action. See footnote 13.

[b] According to DOE, the department has determined that it has EUL authority on the basis of the definition set forth in OMB Circular A-11 (June 2008). DOE officials said that the department has not entered into any EULs using this authority.

[c] While DOI has certain authorities to sell real property, we did not include in the scope of our review lands managed by DOI.

[d] State has used its authority under 22 U.S.C. § 300 to exchange, lease, or license real property outside of the country. According to State, in exceptional cases, the department has relied on this authority to enter into long-term leases to conserve historically significant properties, such as the Talleyrand Building in Paris, France. State's authorization to sell and retain proceeds from the sale of real property applies to its properties located outside of the United States and to properties located within the United States acquired for an exchange with a specified foreign government.

[e] According to State, committee reports accompanying State's appropriations acts routinely require the department to notify Congress through the reprogramming process of the specific planned use of the proceeds of the sale of excess property. Furthermore, State indicated that it routinely includes discussion of the use of proceeds from the sale of real property in its budget justifications and financial plans.

[f] Because USDA's **Agricultural Research Service** received pilot authority to enter into EULs for certain properties effective June 2008, but had not entered into any EULs during our review, we did not include it in the scope of our review.

[g] We are listing the Forest Service separately from USDA because it has authority to sell administrative property and retain the proceeds from the sales, unlike the rest of USDA.

[h] Although the Forest Service has EUL authority, it has not used that authority.

[i] Under certain circumstances, VA can use the proceeds from the sale of former EUL property without further congressional action. See footnote 8.

Authorities are agency-specific and include different provisions. For example, while VA is authorized to enter into EULs for "underutilized" or "unutilized" real property, DOD is authorized to enter into EULs only for "nonexcess" real property.[10] In addition, some agencies must follow the requirements in Title 40 of the United States Code and the McKinney-Vento Homeless Assistance Act before selling real property—and some of these steps may result in the property being disposed of with no proceeds—while other agencies' authorities exempt them from following these requirements.[11] Congress enacted the McKinney-Vento Homeless Assistance Act as a comprehensive federal response to homelessness and enacted the public benefit conveyance (PBC) program as one means of disposing of surplus federal property, whereby state or local governments and certain tax-exempt nonprofit organizations can obtain surplus real property for public uses, such as public heath or educational facilities and public parks and recreational areas. GSA and VA, for example, have the authority to retain proceeds from the sale of real property but must, before offering property for sale, follow the requirements under Title 40 of the United States Code and the McKinney-Vento Homeless Assistance Act. Although DOD also has authority to retain the proceeds from the sale of real property, in certain cases, the department is exempt from following the requirements under Title 40 relating to real property disposition and the McKinney Act.[12] Furthermore, four agencies with the authority to retain proceeds from the sale of real property (DOD, in certain cases;[13] the Forest Service; State; and USPS) have authority to use these proceeds without further congressional action, while two agencies with authority to retain proceeds from the sale of real property, (VA for nonEUL property and GSA) require further congressional action before using them. Figure 1 shows the steps that GSA must follow to sell excess real property and retain the proceeds. (Encl. III illustrates the steps each agency must follow to sell real property.)

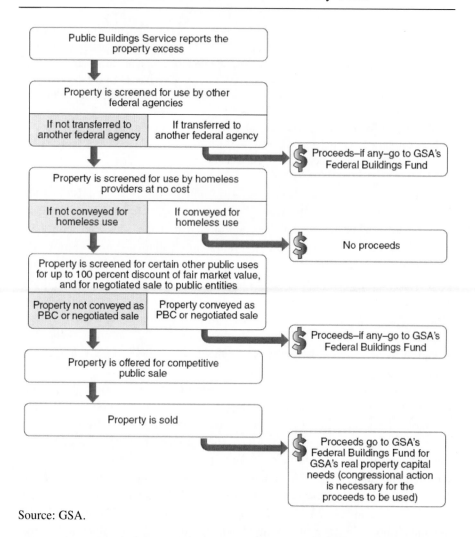

Source: GSA.

Figure 1. GSA's Process for Selling Excess GSA-Controlled Real Property.

By contrast, the Forest Service, State, and USPS do not follow the requirements[14] under Title 40 of the United States Code and the McKinney-Vento Homeless Assistance Act when they wish to sell real property, both reducing the time and effort involved and eliminating instances in which the agency disposes of the property at a discount of up to 100 percent of fair market value. For example, figure 2 shows the steps that State must follow to sell overseas real property.

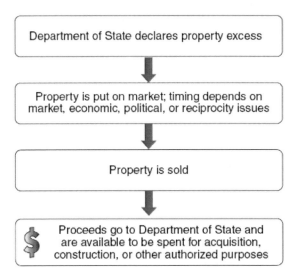

Source: State Department.

Figure 2. State Department's Process for Selling Excess Real Property Located Outside of the United States.

Table 2. Summary of Major Steps that Agencies Follow to Sell Real Property

Agency	Property declared excess	Screened for use by other agencies	Screened for use by homeless	Screened for public benefit use
DOD[a]	Yes	Yes	Yes	Yes
DOD[b,c]	No	No	No	No
GSA	Yes	Yes	Yes	Yes
State	Yes	No	No	No
USDA/Forest Service (for administrative sites)	No	No	No	No
USPS	Yes	No	No	No
VA	Yes	Yes	Yes	Yes

Source: GAO analysis; information provided by the above agencies.

Note: The agencies listed in this table are only those with the authority to retain proceeds from the sale of real property. See enclosure II for the specific authorities provided in this table.

[a] 40 U.S.C. § 572. Under this authority, while the Administrator of GSA is authorized to dispose of DOD property, DOD is the recipient of the proceeds.

[b] 10 U.S.C. § 2854a.

[c] 10 U.S.C. § 2878.

How these proceeds can be spent also varies, as described fully in enclosure II. Table 2 provides a summary of the steps that agencies must follow when selling real property and retaining proceeds.

AGENCIES WITH AUTHORITY TO RETAIN PROCEEDS FROM SALE OF REAL PROPERTY REPORTED SELLING PROPERTY TO VARYING EXTENTS AND USING PROCEEDS FOR PROPERTY MANAGEMENT

Governmentwide data reported to the FRPP were not sufficiently reliable to analyze the extent to which the six agencies with authority to retain proceeds sold real property, due to inconsistent and unreliable reporting. However, these six agencies (DOD, the Forest Service, GSA, State, USPS, and VA) reported selling property to varying extents, with net proceeds ranging from $21 million to $541 million during fiscal years 2006 and 2007. In addition, five agencies (DOD, GSA, State, the Forest Service, and VA) reported using sales proceeds to manage their real property portfolios, such as rental of space, building operations, new construction and acquisition, maintenance, and repairs and alterations, while USPS reported depositing the proceeds into its general fund.

FRPP Data on Real Property Disposal Were Unreliable

According to GSA officials, a data element on disposition (which includes disposition by sale as well as other methods) was added to the FRPP as of fiscal year 2006 to identify unneeded assets that have been removed from the FRPP inventory and to track the volume of disposals to support the strategic goal of right-sizing the federal real property inventory. However, we found inconsistent and unreliable reporting within the disposal data element on the method of disposal and were therefore unable to use the FRPP to analyze the number of sales of real property by agencies with the authority to retain proceeds. For example, the Air Force reported that in fiscal year 2006, it disposed of 4,397 assets by sale, as well as disposing of a number of assets by demolition, federal transfer, or other means. In fiscal year 2007, however, it reported disposing of 12,423 assets, all in the "other" category.[15] Because all of its disposed assets were reported in the "other" category for fiscal year 2007, unlike in the prior fiscal year, we asked Air Force officials about the reasonableness of the data. Air Force officials agreed that the disposal method data summarized and reported in 2007 did not provide disposal information comparable to the level of detail provided in 2006. They said that the primary cause for insufficient data detail has been resolved and that they plan to provide better data in future reporting that more accurately reflects disposal methods.

GSA officials said that every time a new data element is added to the FRPP, the data for that element are likely to be less reliable because agencies need to learn the process and determine how to provide these data. GSA reviews the data submitted by federal agencies and notifies the relevant agencies of any inconsistencies and anomalies. If an agency does not address the inconsistencies or anomalies, GSA will report these to OMB; OMB takes these into account when rating the agencies on their real property management initiative efforts. Nevertheless, these data weaknesses reduce the effectiveness of the FRPP as a tool to enable governmentwide comparisons of real property efforts, such as the effort to reduce the government's portfolio of unneeded property.

Agencies with Authority to Retain Proceeds Reported Selling Real Property to Varying Extent

While we were unable to analyze the governmentwide FRPP database to determine the number of properties sold by agencies with authority to retain proceeds,[16] we asked the six agencies that have authority to retain proceeds from the sale of real property to provide information on the net proceeds received during fiscal years 2006 and 2007. As shown in Table 3, the sales proceeds received by individual agencies in our review ranged from $21 million to $541 million during those 2 years. The highest level of net proceeds for these 2 years was reported by State, largely due to the sale of a facility known as the Navy Annex in London for $494 million.

Table 3. Real Property Sales Proceeds during Fiscal Year 2006 and Fiscal Year 2007, by Agency

Agency	FY 2006 proceeds	FY 2007 proceeds	FY 2006 and FY 2007 total proceeds
DOD	$14,070,949	$41,787,312	$55,858,261
GSA	52,049,163	82,218,326	134,267,489
State	36,035,010	505,145,944	541,180,954
USDA-Forest Service	12,600,000	8,700,000	21,300,000
USPS	91,367,745	201,753,000	293,120,745
VA[a]	22,319,702	0	22,319,702

Sources: DOD, GSA, State, USDA, USPS, and VA.

[a] VA reported that it did not sell any properties through its Capital Asset Fund authority, which authorizes it to sell real property and retain the proceeds, but that it sold one property, shown in this table. The property, the Lakeside VA Medical Center in Chicago, was sold under an EUL agreement after determining that it was no longer needed by the agency. VA's proceeds from the sale of the Lakeside VA Medical Center were $50 million, which included a net present value rental return of $28 million received in 2005 for a 75-year EUL term and an additional $22 million received in 2006, reflected in this table, with the actual closing of the sale of the property.

Former Army housing in Rotterdam, New York

Former Forest Service property, Camp Verde, Arizona

Former federal building in Colorado Springs, Colorado

State Department's former Navy Annex in London, England

Sources: GAO (Army Rotterdam housing, Forest Service Camp Verde, and Colorado Springs federal building); Department of State (London Navy Annex).

Figure 3. Examples of Recently Sold Properties by Agencies with Authority to Retain Proceeds.

Of the six agencies with the authority to sell real property and retain the proceeds, two (State and USPS) use in-house staff to handle the sales, while the other three agencies use GSA for some or all of their sales. Under the Federal Management Regulation, landholding agencies must report excess real property to GSA, which is generally responsible for disposing of real property unless an agency has specific or delegated authority to do so.[17] Property sales handled by GSA are typically sold through auctions. We found that agencies with the authority to retain proceeds from the sale of real property had sold a variety of types of properties in the past several years (see fig. 3).

The sales prices for these recently sold properties varied considerably. While some properties sold for tens of thousands of dollars, one sold for nearly $500 million. Information provided by agency officials on the above properties included the following:

- State's London, England, Navy Annex building sold in 2007 for $494 million, when the London real estate market was at its peak. State Department officials said the sale of this building, which was owned by State but previously used by the Navy, was unique because the sales proceeds from the Navy Annex will be used to build a new embassy in London, rather than used to fund worldwide priorities. State officials provided information on two other examples of sales that they said were more typical, involving the sales of former marine security guard quarters in Cape Town, South Africa, and Quito, Ecuador, in 2008, for $1.1 million and $1.8 million, respectively. The proceeds from those sales were deposited into the department's asset management account to be used for worldwide priorities.
- The Army sold a former Army housing complex in Rotterdam, N.Y., for $1.8 million in 2008. The Army determined this property was excess because it had more housing in the area than it needed to serve its mission. The property, which included several apartment and other buildings on about 8 acres of land, was sold through GSA's online auction for slightly over its appraised value.
- The Forest Service sold two of four parcels of administrative land it offered for sale through GSA's online auction at Camp Verde, Ariz. The first parcel consisted of about 1.6 acres of unimproved land in a residential neighborhood that was sold to private citizens in 2006 for $155,000. The second parcel consisted of about 119 acres of mostly unimproved land that was sold to the town of Camp Verde in 2008 for

$2.4 million. The other two parcels did not sell—a fact that Forest Service officials attributed to a downturn in the real estate market.

- GSA sold a federal building in Colorado Springs, Colo., for $890,000 in 2009. The property consisted of about 1.7 acres of land and a 2-story brick office building built in 1962. Formerly leased to the Air Force, the building had been vacant since December 2007. The property was sold through GSA's online auction.

Agencies Reported Using Sales Proceeds Mainly for Real Property Portfolio Management Purposes

Agencies reported using sale proceeds mainly to help manage their real property portfolios. (Encl. II states how agencies are authorized to use proceeds.) For example, a Forest Service official said that the Forest Service used the proceeds from the Camp Verde sale described above to build a new ranger station at Camp Verde. GSA indicated that its sales proceeds are deposited into GSA's Federal Buildings Fund and used for real property management purposes, such as rental of space, building operations, new construction and acquisition, and repairs and alterations. State Department officials said that the proceeds are collected centrally and used for priorities established by the department's Bureau of Overseas Buildings Operations, including purchasing housing and other properties, constructing new facilities, or rehabilitating existing facilities. USPS officials said that the agency deposits its proceeds from the sale of real property into its general fund, where they become part of USPS's funds for use for agency priorities.

AUTHORITIES AFFECT HOW AGENCIES MANAGE THEIR REAL PROPERTY PORTFOLIO

Agency officials generally said that the authorities to enter into EULs and sell and retain sales proceeds influenced the amount of property that is sold and that they preferred using the authorities that were the least restrictive. The five agencies that do not have the authority to retain proceeds from the sale of real property (DOE; DOI; DOJ; NASA; and USDA, except for the Forest Service), indicated that they would favor having this authority to help manage their real property.

Agencies with Authority for Both EUL and Retention of Sales Proceeds Preferred the Authority Seen as Less Restrictive or More Advantageous

We asked agency officials for their views on the relationship between having the authorities to enter into EULs or to sell real property and retain the sales proceeds and the amount of real property that they sell. Of the six agencies with the authority to retain the proceeds from the sale of real property, officials at five agencies (the Forest Service, GSA, State, USPS, and VA) said that this authority is a strong incentive to sell real property, while officials at one agency, DOD, which had the authority to enter into EULs without offering the properties to the homeless and other federal agencies— said that the authority to retain proceeds is not a strong incentive to sell real property. Officials from five agencies that had authorities to enter into EULs and to retain the proceeds from the sale of real property—GSA, DOD, USDA's Forest Service, USPS, and VA—all stated preferences for the authority seen as less restrictive or more financially advantageous to the agency.[18] State, which also has the authority to enter into EULS and retain the proceeds from the sale of real property, indicated that retaining sales proceeds is the more critical part of its program, but also foresees increasing opportunities for EULs in the future.

DOD and VA officials said that because EULs provide greater incentives, the agencies place greater emphasis on entering into EULs, compared to real property sales. DOD officials emphasized the potential of EULs to serve the department's mission, while stating that its authority to retain proceeds from the sale of real property was not a strong incentive to sell unneeded real property. For example, headquarters DOD officials said that there was little emphasis or potential at DOD for selling excess real property outside of the BRAC process, in part because that process was the department's major initiative to consolidate its real property and had largely taken care of the opportunity to dispose of DOD real property. Disincentives to selling real property, according to DOD officials, include the length of time it can take, since such property must first be offered to other federal agencies, the homeless, and other public benefit uses, and the fact that much DOD property cannot be sold to a private entity for security reasons.

In contrast, DOD officials emphasized the potential for EULs to maximize the utility and value of its real property and to serve its mission needs, and each service has a Web site focused on its existing and proposed EULs. In prior work, we found that EULs are a land use planning tool for DOD that

Army and Air Force are using to gain in-kind services.[19] DOD is authorized to enter into EULs only for nonexcess property, and officials made the distinction between DOD's authority to enter into EULs for nonexcess property and its authority to sell and retain proceeds from the sale of excess real property. However, it was not always clear how DOD determined whether properties were suitable for EULs. For example, Army officials said that the Army considers EULs for properties it would not consider excess because the property creates a buffer zone or security perimeter for an installation. However, the Army entered into a long-term EUL agreement for a mixed-used development of hotel and retail space at Redstone Arsenal, Ala., on Army property that lies outside of the installation's fence and gate. Army officials said that they see the use as compatible with a buffer zone and wanted to maintain some control over the property because a training site is nearby.

Similarly, Air Force officials said that unutilized property may be nonexcess but suitable for an EUL because it is needed for a buffer zone or to avoid encroachment. However, it has proposed a long-term EUL agreement for a hotel/resort development at Emerald Breeze, on 17 acres of Air Force property on an island off the coast of Florida that is not directly adjacent to an installation. Air Force officials said that every EUL agreement states that the lease can be terminated at any time for a national emergency. This allows the Air Force more flexibility than excessing and selling the property, at which point it would lose the right to reacquire it during a national emergency. In addition, an Air Force official said that under the terms of excessing real property, no property is declared excess until a determination has been made that it is excess. Therefore, until that determination is made, the Air Force does not consider that property excess, and it may consider an EUL for that property.

According to VA officials, VA places greater emphasis on entering into EULs, compared to real property sales, in part because VA can enter into EULs with fewer restrictions than under its Capital Asset Fund (CAF) authority to sell and retain proceeds of real property.[20] For example, VA can enter into an EUL without first screening the property for homeless use, as it must for property it wishes to sell under its CAF authority. Moreover, VA has the authority to retain and spend proceeds from EULs without the need for further congressional action, while proceeds retained under CAF authority are subject to further congressional action. [21] In addition, VA is authorized to use EUL proceeds for purposes unrelated to real property, such as providing health care services, which are not permitted under VA's CAF authority. VA officials said that in addition, EULs allow VA to realign its asset portfolio in a way that supports its mission by using EULs to obtain facilities, services, in-kind consideration, or revenue for VA requirements that would otherwise be unavailable or unaffordable. The officials added that local and state government, veterans groups, private partners, and nonprofit entities and other community members potentially benefit when these properties are redeveloped to provide new services and economic opportunities to veterans and the community. VA produces an annual report that discusses and tracks the benefits of its active EULs for the past fiscal year.

VA officials said that although they believe retaining proceeds from the sale of real property is a strong incentive, other factors, such as the needs of veterans' service organizations and the community that are complimentary to VA's mission, are of equal importance. This review and past work found that VA has used authorities, such as EULs, to provide services for veterans, such as homeless housing, drug rehabilitation, and childcare, and to generate revenue. For example, in 2006, at Fort Howard, Md., VA entered into an EUL to use nearly 300,000 square feet of vacant space to develop a retirement community, with priority placement for veterans. Conversely, in another EUL, VA is leasing property in Hillsborough, N.J., called Veterans Industrial Park to a company that subleases the property to a variety of commercial interests needing warehouse or light manufacturing space, as well as the county government. VA officials said that VA did not consider selling this property because, in 1999, when the agency entered into the EUL agreement, it did not have the authority to retain the proceeds from the sale of real property. In addition, GSA had a similar property nearby that the agency had been unable to sell. Other than a small area on the property that is used for VA services to collect and distribute military clothing to homeless veterans, the property lessees are commercial renters who are not providing any direct services to VA. However, VA officials said that it considers such EULs to be in the agency's interest, as VA is receiving about $300,000 to $390,000 a year from rental income that it can use for the agency's priorities.[22] (See fig. 4 for photographs of this property.)

GSA stated that while it has the authority to enter into EULs and sell and retain the proceeds from real property sales, it believes that budget scorekeeping rules under OMB Circular A-11 limit the agency's ability to maximize usage of its EUL authority. In contrast, GSA officials said that the agency's ability to retain proceeds is a strong incentive to dispose of excess real property.[23] From fiscal years 2002 to 2007, it reported 271 assets as excess, helping to avoid more than $600 million of repair and alterations liability and providing GSA with almost $140 million of proceeds, which GSA uses as reinvestment funds for its portfolio of core assets. GSA officials said that it is unlikely that sales proceeds have been seen as an offset to the following year's appropriation. According to GSA officials, the agency's sale of a 1.9 million square-foot facility known as the Middle River Depot in Baltimore County, Md., is a good illustration of how retention of proceeds can motivate GSA to dispose of excess real property and obtain the best value for the government from its real property sales.

Source: GAO.

Figure 4. Veterans Industrial Park, Which Is Generating Lease Payments to VA.

The Middle River Depot, a large warehouse used to build B-26 bombers in World War II, with some associated buildings and land, sold for $37.5 million in 2006. In this case, GSA decided there was no government need for the property, and Congress passed legislation in 2004 for GSA to sell this property and keep the proceeds.[24] The main challenges in marketing and selling the property were community concerns and the state's insistence that the warehouse be covered by a historic easement.[25] GSA officials said that GSA expended considerable time and effort into overcoming these challenges, such as negotiating with the Maryland Historical Trust until it came to an understanding of the basic alterations that would and would not be permitted to the building. GSA subsequently provided this information to prospective bidders. GSA officials said that the agency was motivated to sell the property at the highest possible price because GSA was authorized to retain the proceeds (see fig. 5).

Source: GAO.

Figure 5. Middle River Depot, Md., Sold by GSA in 2006.

Officials at USPS, which has authority to enter into EULs and sell real property and retain proceeds, said that the Postal Service prefers to sell or exchange unneeded property. Officials said that USPS's authority provides the agency with a strong incentive to actively sell or exchange underutilized property that has a high value. Because of the relatively streamlined process to sell real property, compared to other agencies, and its ability to retain and use sales proceeds for any USPS purpose without further congressional action, it has little incentive to enter into EULs and rarely does so. Three former USPS properties that were sold or exchanged in the past few years were initiated by other parties wanting to purchase the building or land. For example, the state of New York approached USPS in the 1990s about purchasing the Farley Building in Manhattan, a historic, 1.4 million-square-foot building across the street from Pennsylvania Station (see fig. 6) to redevelop the building into a new train station to be named the Moynihan Station. USPS sold the Farley Building in 2007 and is in the process of consolidating its operations into two other existing buildings and 250,000 square feet of leaseback space in the Farley building. According to USPS officials, the sale of the Farley building generated financial proceeds to USPS,[26] reduced deferred maintenance costs, consolidated USPS operations into less space overall, and resulted in reduced operating costs. In the other two cases, in Denver and Scottsdale, Ariz., USPS exchanged old post offices with various parties (the city of Denver and a health care company) that sought the postal property and financed new post offices. In both cases, according to USPS's analysis, USPS benefited financially from the transaction, as well as gaining modern and more efficient facilities in return for older ones.

Source: GAO.

Figure 6. Farley Building in New York City, Sold by USPS in 2007.

State Department officials also told us that the authority to retain proceeds is an incentive to dispose of excess real property because it allows the agency to direct resources from the sale of real property to other pressing facilities needs. Although further congressional action is not needed before State may use proceeds from the sales of real property, the department notifies Congress about its intended use of the proceeds in its budget justifications and financial plans.

Officials at the Forest Service, which has authorities to enter into EULs and retain proceeds from the sale of real property, said that the agency's authority to retain proceeds is a strong incentive to sell real property. Officials at this agency described active efforts to analyze their portfolios to find opportunities to sell unneeded real property. Forest Service officials said that since it received authority to retain proceeds in 2001, it has disposed of more properties than before it had the authority.[27] The Forest Service officials said that the agency has benefited in two primary ways from this authority. First, the Forest Service has used proceeds to help address a large backlog of deferred maintenance needs. Second, because it may use proceeds to construct new ranger stations, they said this authority has helped the Forest Service realign its infrastructure to better meet its current mission. Forest Service officials said that a major reason that the authority to keep the proceeds has functioned as an incentive is that the Forest Service's policy is to use proceeds for local or regional priorities where the property is sold. A Forest Service site in Sedona, Ariz., illustrates these benefits. The Forest Service sold a property that had been used as a ranger station, along with some related buildings and land, for $8.4 million to build a new ranger station on another site (see fig. 7). The previous Forest Service ranger station had significant deferred maintenance needs and was on a side street with little traffic in the town of Sedona. According to a Forest Service official, since the new ranger station opened along the main highway to Sedona in April 2008, average monthly visits by the public to the ranger station have increased significantly.

Source: GAO.

Figure 7. New Forest Service Ranger Station in Sedona, Ariz., Funded by Sale of Another Property.

The Forest Service has also sold properties with lower real estate values, including one in Estes Park, Colo., that was sold in August 2008 for $440,000. According to a Forest Service official, the Forest Service no longer ran an office out of Estes Park and did not need the property. In addition, the property had significant maintenance needs. Forest Service officials said that the biggest challenge regarding the sale of this property was the downturn in the housing market, and that the agency faces a similar challenge in selling many other properties under such economic conditions. Even so, the Forest Service considers the disposition a success because it no longer has to maintain this unneeded property and plans to use the proceeds for high-priority deferred maintenance needs.

Agencies without Authority to Retain Proceeds from Real Property Sales Provided Mixed Responses on Whether Such Authority Would Be a Strong Incentive

Officials at the five agencies we contacted that do not have the authority to retain proceeds from the sale of real property (DOE; DOI; DOJ; NASA; and USDA, except for the Forest Service) provided mixed responses when asked about the extent to which such an authority would be an incentive to sell more real property. Officials at the five agencies said their agencies would like to have expanded authorities with which to manage their real property portfolio, including the authority to enter into EULs and retain the proceeds from the sale of real property. However, officials at two of those agencies said that due to challenges such as the security needs or remote locations of most of their properties, it was unlikely there would be a significant number of real properties that were appropriate to sell.

One challenge that agencies face in disposing of real properties is maintaining them until they can be sold. We visited a former USDA Agricultural Research Service laboratory in Phoenix that was for sale. The laboratory was vacated in January 2006 when the staff moved to another location. During our visit, we observed that property had been vandalized and copper from the buildings and part of a greenhouse had been stolen. While GSA is marketing and attempting to sell the property, USDA remains responsible for maintaining it until May 1, 2009, before responsibility is transferred to GSA under certain conditions.

Vandalized USDA laboratory

Destroyed greenhouse

Source: GAO.

Figure 8. Former USDA Laboratory for Sale in Phoenix.

Agencies may also face challenges in exercising their EUL authority. NASA, one agency that does not have the authority to retain proceeds from the sale of real property, has had the authority to enter into EULs at two centers; as of December 31, 2008, a new agencywide authority gives NASA the ability to enter into EULs. In recent work, we found that while NASA has realized some EUL-related financial benefits, among other things—most of which would not have been realized by NASA without this authority—the agency did not have adequate controls in place to ensure accountability and transparency and to protect the government.[28] NASA accepted our recommendations and developed agencywide policy for the administration of EULs and for the financial management of the revenue derived from EULs.[29] NASA officials said that they use EULs, rather than selling the property, when the agency believes the property may be needed in the future or wants to maintain some control over the property.

AGENCY COMMENTS AND OUR EVALUATION

We requested comments on a draft of this report from the Administrator of the General Services Administration; the Administrator of the National Aeronautics and Space Administration; the Attorney General; the Director of the Office of Management and Budget; the Postmaster and Chief Executive Officer of the United States Postal Service; the Secretary of Agriculture; the

Secretary of Defense; the Secretary of Energy; the Secretary of the Interior; the Secretary of State; and the Secretary of Veterans Affairs.

DOE indicated that it agreed with the report's findings and noted that it is important to emphasize that the EUL authority provided to the department under the "Hall Amendment," 42 U.S.C. § 7256(c) is very limited in scope. DOE also indicated that it would greatly benefit from a more expansive and broad EUL authority, similar to the authorities used by DOD. In addition, DOE indicated that, with the increased emphasis on renewable energy as contained in the Energy Policy Act of 2005, legislation that provides expanded authorities to the department would provide the flexibility and tools with which to achieve the goals that are vital to the nation. GSA indicated that it agreed with the report's findings. DOI indicated that the report was a fair summation of the authorities, policies and complex challenges associated with the disposal and transfer of lands and constructed assets. DOE, GSA, NASA, OMB, State, USDA, and VA provided technical clarifications, which we incorporated throughout the report as appropriate. DOD, DOJ, and USPS provided no comments.

David Wise
Director,
Physical Infrastructure Issues

ENCLOSURE I: SCOPE AND METHODOLOGY

Our objective was to review how agencies are using their disposal authorities. To accomplish this, we addressed (1) what authorities the 10 largest real property holding agencies have to enter into enhanced use leases (EUL) or retain proceeds from the sale of real property; (2) the extent to which agencies with authority to retain proceeds sold real property and how they have used the proceeds; and (3) the relationship, if any, between agencies having the authority to enter into EULs or retain sales proceeds and the amount of real property that they retained or sold.

To determine what authorities the 10 largest real property holding agencies have regarding EULs and retention of proceeds from the sale of real property, we first identified the 10 agencies that reported holding real property with the highest values to the Federal Real Property Profile (FRPP) in fiscal year 2007. These 10 agencies include the Department of Agriculture (USDA), Department of Defense (DOD), Department of Energy (DOE), Department of the Interior (DOI), Department of Justice (DOJ), Department of State (State), Department of Veterans Affairs (VA), General Services Administration (GSA), National Aeronautics and Space Administration (NASA), and the United States Postal Service (USPS). For the purposes of this review, the term "real property" does not include real property that DOD has or is planning to dispose of through the Base Realignment and Closure Act (BRAC) process,[30] lands managed by DOI or the Forest Service (except for Forest Service administrative sites), and transfers of individual properties specifically authorized by Congress. We then conducted legal research and interviewed officials at those 10 agencies regarding their authorities to enter into EULs and sell and retain the proceeds from the sales of real property. We also reviewed agencies' asset management plans and real property management policies on issues involving excessing properties, selling properties, and entering into EULs. In addition, we reviewed GSA guidance for federal agencies on declaring excess and selling real property. Furthermore, we reviewed prior GAO reports on real property management, leasing, and selling federal real property.

To determine to what extent agencies with authority to retain proceeds sold real property and how they have used the proceeds, we first obtained and analyzed real property disposition data from the FRPP regarding the 10 agencies. We also interviewed officials from the Office of Management and Budget (OMB) about the reliability of the disposition information contained in the FRPP. After we determined that the FRPP disposition data were unreliable for our purposes, we obtained information on the amount of proceeds from the sales of real property received during fiscal years 2006 and 2007 from the six agencies that are authorized to retain proceeds. We did not independently validate the accuracy of the sales proceeds information that the agencies provided because we considered the data to be sufficiently reliable for our purposes, which was focused more on whether the agencies sold any real property and what they used the proceeds for, rather than an accurate accounting of the funds received for those properties. In addition, we interviewed officials from the 10 agencies about the processes that they follow in disposing of real property and their recent real property sales, including the reasons for selling the properties, how they were marketed, and the challenges faced.

To determine the relationship, if any, between agencies having the authority to enter into EULs or retain sales proceeds and the amount of real property that they retained or sold, we interviewed agency officials about the factors they considered in deciding whether or how to dispose of unneeded real property, including the authorities available. We also visited a VA EUL site in Hillsborough, N.J., and interviewed officials from the property management and leasing companies about the agreement and how the property was being used.

To help address the second and third research questions, we also visited federal properties that had been sold or were for sale in Camp Verde, Ariz.; Colorado Springs, Colo.; Denver; Estes Park, Colo.; Glendale, Ariz.; Guilderland, N.Y.; Loveland, Colo.; Middle River, Md.; New York; Peoria, Ariz., Rotterdam, N.Y.; Scotia, N.Y.; Scottsdale, Ariz.; Sedona, Ariz.; and Tucson, Ariz. During the site visits, we interviewed officials involved in the sales, including officials from the agencies that held the properties; GSA; and, when available, the buyers. We also obtained information from the agencies that were authorized to retain the sales proceeds on how they used the proceeds.

ENCLOSURE II: SELECTED REAL PROPERTY AUTHORITIES AND RETENTION OF PROCEEDS AUTHORITIES FOR MAJOR REAL PROPERTY HOLDING AGENCIES

Real property holding agency	Authority	Description of authority
DOD[a]	Leases of Non-Excess Property of Military Departments 10 U.S.C. § 2667	The Secretary of a military department is authorized to lease nonexcess real property under the control of the department that is not needed for public use if the Secretary considers the lease to be advantageous to the United States and upon such terms that will promote the national defense or be in the public interest. The term of the lease may not be more than 5 years, unless the Secretary determines the term should be longer to promote the national defense or to be in the public interest. Lease payments shall be in cash or in-kind consideration for an amount not less than fair market value.

Real property holding agency	Authority	Description of authority
		In-kind consideration includes maintenance, protection, alteration, repair, or environmental restoration of property or facilities; construction of new facilities; providing facilities; or providing or paying for utility services.
DOD	Retention of Proceeds/ Leases of Non-Excess Property of Military Departments 10 U.S.C. § 2667	Proceeds from leases of a military department are deposited into a special account in the Treasury and are available to the Secretary of that military department for such activities as maintenance, protection, alteration, or environmental restoration of property or facilities; construction of new facilities; lease of facilities; or payment of utility services. At least 50 percent of the proceeds received shall be available for activities at the military installations where the proceeds are derived. Prior to fiscal year 2005, any amounts deposited in a special account from the disposition of property were subject to expenditure, as provided in an appropriation act. Beginning in fiscal year 2005, any amounts deposited into a special account from the disposition of property are appropriated and available for expenditure.[b]
DOD	Conveyance of Damaged or Deteriorated Military Family Housing 10 U.S.C. § 2854a	The Secretary concerned is authorized to convey any family housing facility, including the real property associated with the facility, which due to damage or deterioration is in a condition that is uneconomical to repair. The person to whom the facility is conveyed shall pay an amount equal to the fair market value of the facility conveyed, including any real property conveyed along with the facility.[c]
DOD	Retention of Proceeds/ Conveyance of Damaged or Deteriorated Military Family Housing 10 U.S.C. § 2854a	Proceeds of any conveyance of a damaged or deteriorated military family housing facility shall be credited to the Department of Defense Housing Improvement Funds, 10 U.S.C. § 2883, and shall be available, without any further appropriation,

Enclosure II. (Continued)

Real property holding agency	Authority	Description of authority
		to construct family housing units to replace the family housing facility conveyed under this section; to repair or restore existing military family housing; and to reimburse the Secretary concerned for the costs incurred by the Secretary in conveying the family housing facility.
DOD	Conveyance or Lease of Existing Property and Facilities 10 U.S.C. § 2878	The Secretary concerned is authorized to convey or lease property or facilities, including ancillary supporting facilities to eligible entities at such consideration the Secretary concerned considers appropriate for the purposes of the alternative authority for acquisition and improvement of military housing and to protect the interests of the United States.[d]
DOD	Retention of Proceeds/ Conveyance or Lease of Existing Property and Facilities 10 U.S.C. § 2883	Proceeds from the conveyance or lease of property or facilities under 10 U.S.C. § 2878 shall be credited to the Department of Defense Housing Improvement Funds. Proceeds may be used to carry out activities with respect to the alternative authority for the acquisition and improvement of military housing, including activities required in connection with the planning, execution, and administration of contracts subject to such amounts as provided in appropriation acts.
DOD	General Services Administration's (GSA) Disposal of Real Property Under a Military Department's Control that is Excess to the Department's Needs 40 U.S.C. § 572	The Administrator of GSA is authorized to dispose of property under the control of a military department that is not subject to closure or realignment and is excess to the department's needs.[e]

Real property holding agency	Authority	Description of authority
DOD	Retention of Proceeds/ GSA's Disposal of Real Property Under a Military Department's Control that is Excess to the Department's Needs 40 U.S.C. § 572	Proceeds from the disposition of the property are deposited into a special account in the Treasury, less expenses incurred by GSA for the disposition. Fifty percent of the proceeds are available for facility maintenance and repair or environmental restoration at the military installation where the property was located, and 50 percent of the proceeds are available for facility maintenance and repair or for environmental restoration by the military department that had jurisdiction over the property. Prior to fiscal year 2005, any amounts deposited into a special account from the disposition of property were subject to expenditure, as provided in an appropriation act. Beginning in fiscal year 2005, any amounts deposited in a special account from the disposition of property are appropriated and available for expenditure.[f]
DOE	Leasing of Excess Property 42 U.S.C. § 7256	The Secretary of Energy is authorized to lease excess real property located at a DOE facility that is to be closed or reconfigured and is not needed by DOE at the time the lease is entered into if the Secretary considers the lease to be appropriate to promote national security or is in the public interest. The term of the lease may be up to 10 years, with an option to renew the lease for another 10 years, if the Secretary determines that a renewal of the lease will promote national security or be in the public interest. Lease payments may be in cash or in-kind consideration for an amount less than fair market value. In kind consideration may include services relating to the protection and maintenance of the leased property.
DOE	Retention of Proceeds/ Leasing of Excess Property 42 U.S.C. § 7256	To the extent provided in advance in appropriations acts, the Secretary is authorized to use the funds received as rents to cover administrative expenses of

Enclosure II. (Continued)

Real property holding agency	Authority	Description of authority
		the lease, maintenance and repair of the leased property, or environmental restoration activities at the facility where the leased property is located.
GSA	Disposition of Real Property 40 U.S.C. § 543	The Administrator of GSA is authorized to dispose of surplus real property by sale, exchange, lease, permit, or transfer for cash, credit, or other property.
GSA	Conveyance of Property Consolidated Appropriations Act of 2005, P.L. No. 108-447, § 412, 118 Stat. 2809, 3259 (2004)	The Administrator of GSA, notwithstanding any other provision of law, is authorized to convey by sale, lease, exchange, or otherwise, including through leaseback arrangements, real and related personal property, or interests therein.
GSA	Retention of Proceeds/ Conveyance of Property Consolidated Appropriations Act of 2005, P.L. No. 108-447, § 412, 118 Stat. 2809, 3259 (2004)	Net proceeds from the disposition of real property are deposited in GSA's Federal Buildings Fund (FBF) and are used for GSA real property capital needs to the extent provided in appropriations acts.
NASA	Enhanced Use Lease Real Property Demonstration 42 U.S.C. § 2459j	The Administrator of NASA is authorized to enter into a lease agreement with any person or entity, including federal, state, or local governments, with regard to any real property at two NASA centers. The lease shall be for fair market value and payments may be in cash. Prior to December 31, 2008, NASA could have accepted for lease payments in-kind consideration such as construction, maintenance, or improvement of facilities, or providing services to NASA such as launch and payload processing services.[g]
NASA	Retention of Proceeds/ Enhanced Use Lease Real Property Demonstration 42 U.S.C. § 2459j	Cash consideration received for the lease is to be used to cover the full costs to NASA in connection with the lease and shall remain available until expended. Thirty-five percent of any remaining cash shall be deposited in a capital asset account

Real property holding agency	Authority	Description of authority
		available for maintenance, capital revitalization, and improvements of real property assets under the jurisdiction of the Administrator and shall remain available until expended. The remaining 65 percent of the cash shall be available to the respective center or facility engaged in the lease of nonexcess real property and shall remain available until expended for maintenance, capital revitalization, and improvements of real property assets at the respective center or facility, subject to the concurrence of the Administrator.
NASA	Lease of Non-Excess Property 42 U.S.C. § 2459j	Effective December 31, 2008, the Administrator of NASA is authorized to enter into a lease agreement with any person or entity, including federal, state, or local governments, with regard to any nonexcess real property under the jurisdiction of the Administrator. The lease shall be for cash consideration of the fair market value as determined by the Administrator.[h]
NASA	Retention of Proceeds/ Lease of Non-Excess Property 42 U.S.C. § 2459j	Cash consideration received for the lease is to be used to cover the full costs to NASA in connection with the lease and shall remain available until expended. Thirty-five percent of any remaining cash shall be deposited into a capital asset account available for maintenance, capital revitalization, and improvements of real property assets under the jurisdiction of the
		Administrator and shall remain available until expended. The remaining 65 percent of the cash shall be available to the respective center or facility engaged in the lease of non-excess real property and shall remain available until expended for maintenance, capital revitalization, and improvements of real property assets at the respective center or facility, subject to the concurrence of the Administrator.

Enclosure II. (Continued)

Real property holding agency	Authority	Description of authority
		Effective December 31, 2008, no funds may be used for daily operating costs.
State	Disposition of Property 22 U.S.C. § 300	The Secretary of State is authorized to sell, exchange, lease, or license any property or property interest acquired in foreign countries for diplomatic and consular establishments.
State	Retention of Proceeds/ Disposition of Property 22 U.S.C. § 300	Proceeds from the disposition of properties are applied toward acquisition, construction, or other purposes authorized by this chapter; Foreign Service Buildings; or deposited into the Foreign Service Buildings Funds, as in the judgment of the Secretary may best serve the government's interest.
USDA	Enhanced Use Lease Authority Pilot Program 7 U.S.C. § 3125a note[i]	The Secretary of Agriculture is authorized to establish a pilot program and lease nonexcess real property at the Beltsville Agricultural Research Center and the National Agricultural Library to any individual or entity, including agencies or instrumentalities of State or local governments, if the Secretary determines that the lease is consistent with, and will not adversely affect, the mission of the agency administering the property; will enhance the use of the property; will not permit any portion of the property or facility to be used for the public retail or wholesale sale of merchandise or
		residential development; will not permit the construction or modification of facilities financed by nonfederal sources to be used by an agency, except for incidental use; and will not include any property or facility required for any agency purpose without prior consideration of the needs of the agency. Consideration for any lease shall be for fair market value and for cash.

Real property holding agency	Authority	Description of authority
		The Secretary is authorized to enter into leases until June 18, 2013, and the term of the lease shall not exceed 30 years.
USDA	Retention of Proceeds/ Enhanced Use Lease Authority Pilot Program 7 U.S.C. § 3125a note	Consideration for leases shall be deposited in a capital asset account, which is available until expended, without further appropriation, for maintenance, capital revitalization, and improvements to the department's properties and facilities at the Beltsville Agricultural Research Center and the National Agricultural Library.
USDA-Forest Service	Conveyance of Forest Service Administrative Sites 16 U.S.C. § 580d notej	The Secretary of Agriculture is authorized to convey administrative sites of 40 acres or less under the Secretary's jurisdiction by sale, lease, exchange, or combination of sale and exchange. An administrative site is defined as a facility or improvement, including curtilage, that was acquired or is used specifically for purposes of administration of the National Forest System (NFS); any federal land associated with a facility or improvement that was acquired or specifically used for purposes of administration of Forest Service activities and underlies or abuts the facility or improvement; or not more than 10 isolated, undeveloped parcels per fiscal year of not more than 40 acres each that were acquired or used for purposes of administration of Forest Service activities, but are not being so utilized such as vacant lots outside of the proclaimed boundary of a unit of NFS. This conveyance authority, which would have expired on September 30, 2008, was extended until March 6, 2009.k
USDA-Forest Service	Retention of Proceeds/ Conveyance of Forest Service Administrative Sites 16 U.S.C. § 580d note	Proceeds from the conveyance of administrative sites are available to the Secretary of Agriculture, until expended and without further appropriation, to pay any necessary and incidental costs in connection with the acquisition,

Enclosure II. (Continued)

Real property holding agency	Authority	Description of authority
		improvement, maintenance, reconstruction, or construction of a facility or improvement for the NFS, and the conveyance of administrative sites, including commissions or fees for brokerage services.
USPS	Real Property Authorities 39 U.S.C. § 401(5)	The Postal Service is authorized to acquire in any legal manner, real property or any interest therein, as it deems necessary or convenient in the transaction of its business and to hold, maintain, sell, lease, or otherwise dispose of such property or any interest therein.
USPS	Real Property Authorities 39 U.S.C. § 401(6)	The Postal Service is authorized to construct, operate, lease, and maintain buildings, facilities, or equipment, and to make other improvements on any property owned or controlled by it.
USPS	Retention of Proceeds/ Real Property Authorities 39 U.S.C. §§ 2003 and 2401	Proceeds are deposited into the Postal Service Fund and remain available to the Postal Service without fiscal year limitation to carry out the purposes, functions, and powers authorized by Title 39, Postal Service. All revenues received by the Postal Service are appropriated to the Postal Service.
VA	Transfer Authority – Capital Asset Fund 38 U.S.C. § 8118	The Secretary of VA is authorized to transfer real property under VA's control or custody to another department or agency of the United States, to a state or political subdivision of a state, or to any public or private entity, including an Indian tribe
		until November 30, 2011. The property must be transferred for fair market value, unless it is transferred to a homeless provider. Property under this authority cannot be disposed of until the Secretary determines that the property is no longer needed by the department in carrying out its functions and is not suitable for use for the provision of services to homeless

Real property holding agency	Authority	Description of authority
		veterans by the department under the McKinney-Vento Act or by another entity under VA's EUL authority.
VA	Retention of Proceeds/ Transfer Authority 38 U.S.C. § 8118	Proceeds from the transfer of real property are deposited into the VA Capital Asset Fund and, to the extent provided in advance in appropriations acts, may be used for property transfer costs such as demolition, environmental remediation, and maintenance and repair; costs associated with future transfers of property under this authority; costs associated with enhancing medical care services to veterans by improving, renovating, replacing, updating, or establishing patient care facilities through minor construction projects; and costs associated with the transfer or adaptive use of property that is under the Secretary's jurisdiction and listed on the National Register of Historic Places.
VA	Enhanced Used Leases 38 U.S.C. §§ 8161-8169	The Secretary of VA is authorized to enter into leases for up to 75 years with public and private entities for underutilized and unutilized real property that is under the Secretary's jurisdiction or control. EULs shall be for "fair consideration," (i.e., cash and/or in-kind consideration, such as construction, repair, or remodeling of department facilities); providing office space, storage, or other usable space; and providing good or services to the department. The authority to enter into EULs terminates on December 31, 2011.
VA	Retention of Proceeds/ Enhanced Use Leases 38 U.S.C. § 8165	Expenses incurred by the Secretary of VA in connection with EULs will be deducted from the proceeds of the lease and may be used to reimburse the account from which the funds were used to pay such expenses. The proceeds can be used for any expenses incurred in the development of additional EULs. Remaining funds shall be deposited into the VA Medical Care Collections Fund

Enclosure II. (Continued)

Real property holding agency	Authority	Description of authority
		(see authority below for additional uses of EUL proceeds).
VA	Retention of Proceeds/ Enhanced Use Lease Property Consolidated Security, Disaster Assistance, and Continuing Appropriations Act of 2009, P.L. No. 110-329, § 213, 122 Stat. 3574, 3711 (2008)	At the Secretary's discretion, proceeds or revenues derived from EUL activities, including disposal, may be deposited into the "Construction, Major Projects" and "Construction Minor Projects" accounts and used for construction, alterations, and improvements of any VA medical facility.[1]
VA	Disposal of Enhanced Use Lease Property 38 U.S.C. § 8164	If the Secretary of VA determines during the term of an EUL or within 30 days after the end of the lease term that the property is no longer needed by the department, the Secretary is authorized to initiate an action to dispose of the property.
VA	Retention of Proceeds/ Disposal of Enhanced Use Lease Property 38 U.S.C. § 8165	Funds received by VA from a disposal of an EUL property are deposited into the VA Capital Asset Fund and may be used to the extent provided for in appropriations acts for property transfer costs such as demolition, environmental remediation, maintenance, and repair; costs associated with future transfers of property under this authority; costs associated with enhancing medical care services to veterans by improving, renovating, replacing, updating or establishing patient care facilities through construction projects;
		and costs associated with the transfer or adaptive use of property which is under the Secretary's jurisdiction and listed on the National Register of Historic Places (see authority below for additional uses of EUL disposal proceeds).

Real property holding agency	Authority	Description of authority
VA	Retention of Proceeds/ Disposal of Enhanced Use Lease Property Consolidated Security, Disaster Assistance, and Continuing Appropriations Act of 2009, P.L. No. 110-329, § 213, 122 Stat. 3574, 3711 (2008)	At the Secretary's discretion, proceeds or revenues derived from EUL activities, including disposal, may be deposited into the "Construction, Major Projects" and "Construction Minor Projects" accounts and used for construction, alterations, and improvements of any VA medical facility.

Source: GAO analysis.

Note: This list is not intended to be an all inclusive list of an agency's authorities. Furthermore, this list specifically excludes DOD authorities to sell or lease property under a base closure or realignment, lands managed by DOI or the Forest Service, except for Forest Service administrative sites and the Agricultural Research Service's EUL pilot program, and transfers of individual properties authorized by Congress.

[a] Our review of DOD did not include real property at a military installation designated for closure or realignment under a base closure law. Therefore, for purposes of this appendix we have excluded DOD authorities relating to base closure or realignment. Additionally, while some authorities in this enclosure, such as 10 U.S.C. § 2667, contain subsections relating to base closure and realignment, for purposes of this enclosure we are referring to the other subsections of the statute.

[b] Department of Defense Appropriations Act of Fiscal Year 2005, P.L. No. 108-287, § 8034, 118 Stat. 951, 978 (2004).

[c] This authority does not apply to family housing facilities located at military installations approved for closure under a base closure law or family housing activities located at an installation outside the United States at which the Secretary of Defense terminates operations. See 10 U.S.C. § 2854a(a)(2).

[d] This authority does not apply to property or facilities located on or near a military installation approved for closure under a base closure law. See 10 U.S.C. § 2878(b).

[e] This authority does not apply to property at a military installation designated for closure or realignment pursuant to a base closure law. See 40 U.S.C. § 572(b)(2)(B)(ii).

[f] Department of Defense Appropriations Act of Fiscal Year 2005, P.L. No. 108-287, § 8034, 118 Stat. 951, 978 (2004).

[g] NASA was provided EUL authority in 2003. See the Consolidated Appropriations Resolution of FY 2003, P.L. No. 108-7, §418, 117 Stat. 11, 525-526 (2003).

[h] The Consolidated Appropriations Act for FY 2008, P.L. No. 110-161, § 533, 121 Stat. 1844, 1931-1932 (2007), amended NASA's EUL authority at 42 U.S.C. § 2459j to include any NASA non-excess real property, rather than just nonexcess real property at two NASA facilities. P.L. No. 110-161 also amended NASA's EUL authority at 42 U.S.C. § 2459j to allow for cash consideration only when entering into a lease and to prohibit any cash received for the EUL from being used for daily operating costs. These amendments are effective as of December 31, 2008.

[i] This pilot program was enacted in the Food, Conservation, and Energy Act of 2008, P.L. No. 110-246, § 7409, 112 Stat. 1651, 2014-2016 (2008).

^j This authority, the Forest Service Facility Realignment and Enhancement Act, was enacted in 2005 as part of P.L. No. 109-54, Title V, §§ 501-505, 119 Stat. 499, 559-563 (2005).

^k Consolidated Security, Disaster Assistance, and Continuing Appropriations Act of FY 2009, P.L. No. 110-329, §149, 122 Stat. 3574, 3581 (2008).

^l This provision has been included in numerous appropriations acts. See the Consolidated Security, Disaster Assistance, and Continuing Appropriations Act of FY 2009, P.L. No. 110-329, § 213,110 Stat. 3574, 3711 (2008); the Consolidated Appropriations Act of FY 2008, P.L. No. 110-161, § 213, 121 Stat. 1844, 2270 (2007); the Consolidated Appropriations Act of FY 2005, P. L. No. 108-447, § 117, 118 Stat. 2809, 3293 (2004); and the Consolidated Appropriations Act of FY 2004, P.L. 108-199, § 117, 118 Stat. 3, 371 (2004).

ENCLOSURE III: FLOW CHARTS OF AGENCIES' REAL ESTATE DISPOSAL PROCESSES

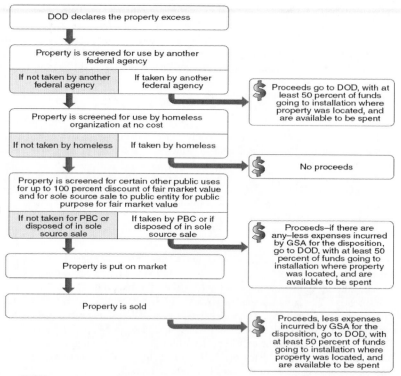

Source: DOD.

Note: This flow chart reflects the disposal process under 40 U.S.C. § 572.

Figure 9. DOD's Real Property Disposal Process.

Source: USDA.

Figure 10. Forest Service's Real Property Disposal Process.

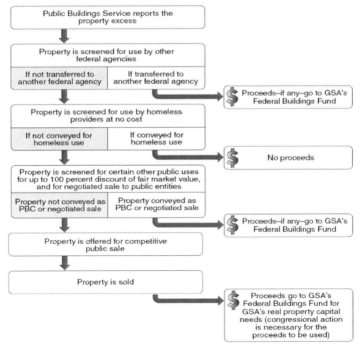

Source: GSA.

Figure 11. GSA's Process for Selling Excess GSA-Controlled Real Property.

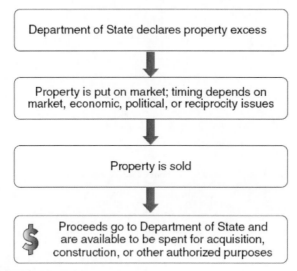

Source: State Department.

Figure 12. State Department's Real Property Disposal Process.

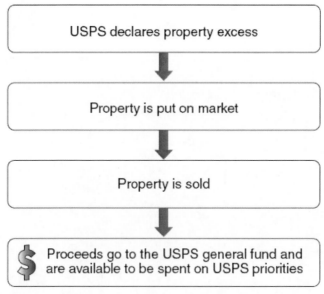

Source: USPS.

Figure 13. U.S. Postal Service's Real Property Disposal Process.

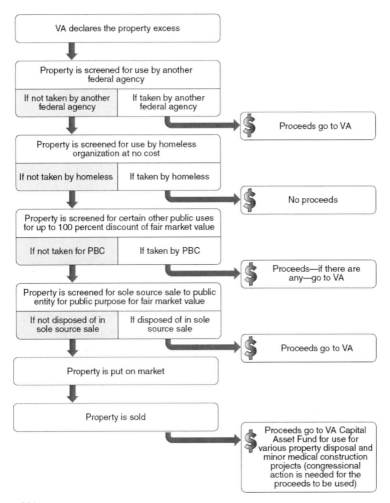

Source: VA.
Note: If sold by GSA, the proceeds are given to the U.S. Treasury.

Figure 14. VA's Real Property Disposal Process.

End Notes

[1] Section 102 of Title 40 of the United States Code defines "excess property" as property under the control of a federal agency that the federal agency determines is not required to meet the agency's needs or responsibilities. The General Services Administration's Federal Management Regulation defines "not utilized property" as an entire property or portion of a property that is not occupied for current program purposes of the accountable agency or

property that is occupied in caretaker status only. The regulation defines "underutilized property" as an entire property or portion of a property that is used only at irregular periods or intermittently by the accountable agency or property that is being used for the agency's current program purposes that can be satisfied with only a portion of the property (41 C.F.R. §§102-75.45 & 75.50).

[2] GAO, *High-Risk Series: An Update,* GAO-03-119 (Washington, D.C.: January 2003) and *High-Risk Series: An Update,* GAO-09-271 (Washington, D.C.: January 2009).

[3] Executive Order No. 13327, Feb. 4, 2004.

[4] Under the BRAC process, the Secretary of Defense is authorized to close certain military bases and dispose of property. In the scope of our review, we included real property disposed of by DOD through its authority to convey or lease existing property and facilities outside of the BRAC process.

[5] Because USDA's Agricultural Research Service (ARS) received pilot authority to enter into EULs for certain properties effective June 2008, but had not entered into any EULs during our review, we did not include ARS in the scope of our review.

[6] DOI has authorities that permit it to sell certain real property and retain the proceeds, but we did not include lands managed by DOI in our review.

[7] According to State, committee reports accompanying State's appropriations acts routinely require the department to notify Congress through the reprogramming process of the specific planned use of the proceeds of the sale of excess property. Furthermore, State indicated that it routinely includes discussion of the use of proceeds from the sale of real property in its budget justifications and financial plans.

[8] VA has two authorities under which it can sell real property and retain the proceeds. Under the first authority, the Capital Asset Fund (CAF) at 38 U.S.C. § 8118, VA can sell real property subject to certain restrictions. The proceeds are deposited in the CAF which are subject to further congressional action. Under the second authority, VA can sell real property related to an EUL that is no longer needed by the department. When this property is sold, under 38 U.S.C. § 8165, the proceeds are deposited in the CAF which would require further congressional action. Alternatively, in its annual appropriations act, the Secretary of VA is authorized to deposit proceeds from EULs, including sale proceeds, into VA's major or minor construction accounts, and use these proceeds for construction, alteration, and improvement projects. While congressional action is needed to pass VA's annual appropriation acts, no further congressional action is needed for VA to spend these proceeds.

[9] Since these agencies lack disposal authority, GSA would dispose of these agencies' excess property and the proceeds from the disposal would be deposited into the U.S. Treasury.

[10] Land that DOD classifies as "underutilized" or "not utilized" may not necessarily be considered "excess property." Pursuant to 40 U.S.C. §102, "excess property" is defined as property under the control of a federal agency that the head of the agency determines is not required to meet the agency's needs or responsibilities. Therefore, a parcel of DOD real property could potentially be underutilized, yet still not be excess, because it is required to meet certain DOD needs or responsibilities.

[11] Title 40 of the United States Code governs the disposal of most federal real property. When a federal agency no longer needs a property to carry out its mission responsibilities, the property is reported as excess and is offered to other federal agencies for use. If another federal agency does not have a need for the property, it is considered surplus to the federal government. Pursuant to the McKinney-Vento Homeless Assistance Act, the Department of Housing and Urban Development then reviews the property to determine if it is suitable for

homeless use. If the property is considered suitable for homeless use, it is first made available for homeless use consideration at 100 percent discount of fair market value by state or local governments and certain tax-exempt nonprofit organizations for 60 days prior to any other public benefit uses. If the property is not considered suitable or if there is no interest in the property, it becomes available for other public benefit uses through the public benefit conveyance (PBC) program. In the PBC program, state or local governments and certain tax-exempt nonprofit organizations can obtain the property for an approved public benefit use, such as education or parks and recreation. Properties can be conveyed to grantees at a discount of up to 100 percent of fair market value.

[12] 10 U.S.C. §§ 2854a and 2878.

[13] DOD has several different authorities to retain proceeds from the sale of real property. Under 40 U.S.C. § 572, the Administrator of GSA is authorized to dispose of property under the control of a military department that is not subject to closure and is excess to the department's needs. Proceeds from the sale are deposited into a special account in the Treasury for DOD and, since fiscal year 2005, are available for expenditure without being subject to further congressional action. Also under 10 U.S.C. § 2854a, DOD is authorized to convey damaged or deteriorated military family housing and to retain the proceeds for use without further congressional action. Under 10 U.S.C. § 2878, the Secretary is authorized to convey property or facilities for the military housing privatization initiative and the use of the proceeds is subject to further congressional action.

[14] Under 40 U.S.C. § 113(e)(7), State is exempt from following Title 40 requirements regarding the sale of excess real property. Furthermore, because State's properties are located outside of the United States, the McKinney-Vento Homeless Assistance Act does not apply. USPS's own authorities also exempt USPS from these requirements. The Forest Service interprets its authority to convey administrative sites under 16 U.S.C. § 580d note to exempt it from the requirements under Title 40 of the United States Code and the McKinney-Vento Homeless Assistance Act.

[15] FRPP data are requested by constructed asset, and one "property" may include many constructed assets.

[16] Although we asked the agencies to provide data on the number of properties sold during fiscal years 2006 and 2007, we are not reporting them because the methods that the agencies used to count the number of properties were not comparable.

[17] 41 C.F.R. § 102-75.115.

[18] In a 2003 report, we found that outleasing historic properties under the National Historic Preservation Act, 16 U.S.C. § 470h-3, promotes certain benefits such as the restoration of historic buildings, but that it is unclear whether selling such properties would accomplish the same purpose with greater economic benefit to the taxpayer. See GAO, *Budget Issues: Alternative Approaches to Finance Federal Capital*, GAO-03-1011 (Washington, D.C.: Aug. 21, 2003). At times, these outleases, like some EULs, have been long-term leases for commercial development. For example, in Washington, D.C., GSA leased the U.S. Tariff Building, which had been vacant for a number of years, to the Kimpton Hotel and Restaurant Group, Inc. for 60 years. This group restored the building, converting it into a luxury hotel.

[19] GAO, *Defense Infrastructure: Services' Use of Land Use Planning Authorities,* GAO-08-850 (Washington, D.C.: July 23, 2008).

[20] VA's CAF authority at 38 U.S.C. §8118 established a revolving fund and granted the Secretary the authority to transfer, sell, or exchange real property and deposit funds into the CAF.

CAF funds may be used for property transfer costs, minor medical construction projects, or historic VA properties.

[21] Under 38 U.S.C. §8165, VA is authorized to spend EUL proceeds without further congressional action for EUL expenses and veterans' health care services. Additionally, in its annual appropriations act, the Secretary of VA is authorized to deposit EUL proceeds into VA's major or minor construction accounts, and use them for construction, alteration, and improvement projects. While congressional action is needed to pass VA's annual appropriation acts, no further congressional action is needed for VA to spend these proceeds.

[22] According to VA officials, VA also has a profit participation agreement for the EUL based on the lessee's net income. In 2007, VA received proceeds from the profit participation for the first time in the amount of about $32,000.

[23] GSA received permanent authority to sell and retain the net proceeds from real property sales in fiscal year 2005. Section 412 of P.L. No. 108-447, 118 Stat. 2809, 3259 (2004).

[24] Section 407 of P.L. No. 108-447, 118 Stat. 2809, 3258 (2004). Although we excluded from our legal research transfers of individual properties authorized by Congress, we visited this property upon GSA's recommendation.

[25] Under a historic easement, the future owner would have to obtain approval from the Maryland Historical Trust for any changes to the interior or exterior of the building.

[26] A USPS official said that the Postal Service originally agreed to sell the Farley building for $230 million, including $55 million in a deferred purchase price that will not be paid until the commercial component of the development is built. The official said that as of January 2009, USPS has received $195 million, which is $20 million more than was expected because of inflation and other factors.

[27] In 2001, the Forest Service received authority for a pilot program to convey excess Forest Service administrative structures and to retain the proceeds from those sales. This 2001 authority was replaced with its current authority in 2005.

[28] GAO, *NASA: Enhanced Use Leasing Program Needs Additional Controls,* GAO-07-306R (Washington, D.C.: Mar. 1, 2007).

[29] NASA indicated that the initial agencywide administrative policy, which was published in July 2007, has since been updated to reflect the legislation and changes to NASA's EUL authority. According to NASA, the most recent update was sent to all NASA centers in December 2008 and the agency's Office of the Chief Financial Officer sent out financial policy for EUL revenue in May 2008. NASA indicated that these actions were taken to address the concerns expressed in the GAO review and have ensured accountability and transparency and protection for the government.

[30] Under the BRAC process, the Secretary of Defense is authorized to close certain military bases and dispose of property. In the scope of our review, we included real property disposed of by DOD through its authority to convey or lease existing property and facilities outside of the BRAC process.

INDEX

E

F

P

Q

R

S

T

U

V

W

Y